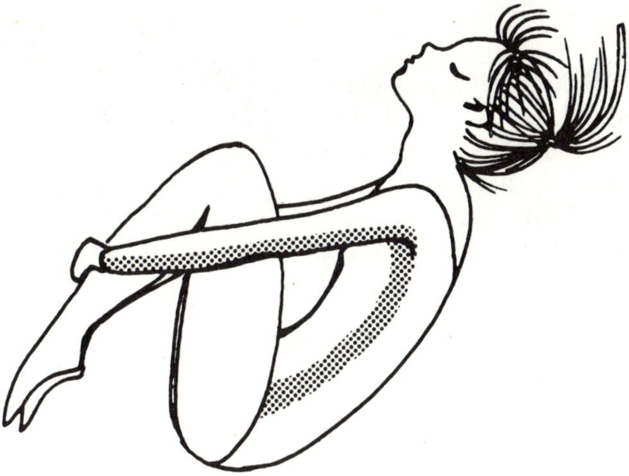

Contents

This book is dedicated to Nadia Comaneci and to the coaches who taught her how to best use her remarkable abilities.

The author wishes to acknowledge with thanks the assistance of the distinguished physical fitness authority and gymnastics enthusiast, Nicholas Kounovsky, for providing the motion pictures of Nadia competing in New York, upon which the drawings in this book are based; and of Radu Teodorescu, for research and statistical information.

Nadia

The Success Secrets of the
Amazing Romanian Gymnast

BY ION GRUMEZA

Edited by Fred Kerner

Drawings by Lisa Craig Wesson

Photographs by
Bruce Curtis
Bob Greene
Joe DiMaggio
and others

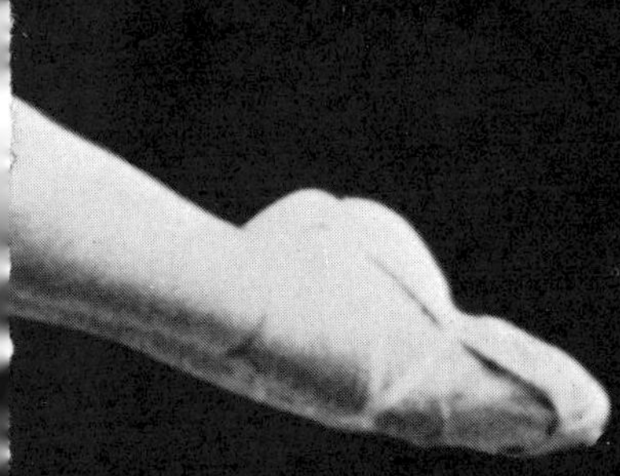

Robson Books

FIRST PUBLISHED IN GREAT BRITAIN IN 1977 BY ROBSON BOOKS LTD., 28 POLAND STREET, LONDON W1V 3DB.

Designer: Ernst Reichl

British Library Cataloguing in Publication Data

Grumeza, Ion
Nadia.
1. Comaneci, Nadia 2. Gymnastics – Biography
I. Title
796.4'1'0924 GV460.2.C/
ISBN 0–86051–010–7

Printed and bound in Great Britain by Redwood Burn Limited, Trowbridge & Esher

Foreword

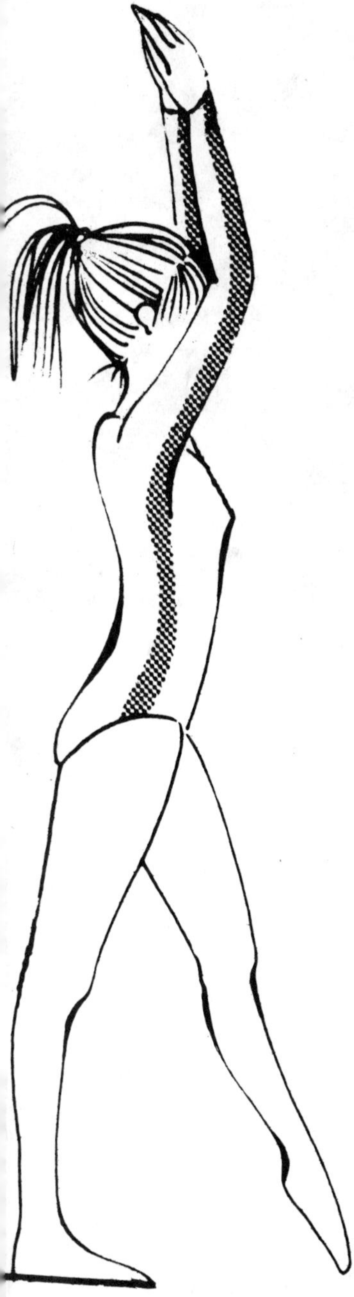

On the first day of the Twenty-First Olympiad in Montreal, a television reporter was asking a random sampling of people on the street how they pronounced a name that he had written on a piece of paper. Everyone was puzzled by the unusual-looking name. Each tried to read the name, and the range of sounds was all but endless: "Comanesky," "Comanov," "Comanician," "Comanenisi," "Caminsky." One person, very sure of himself, pronounced the unfamiliar name: "Comanition!"

The reporter asked, "Doesn't anybody know this name?" The answer was universal: "Never heard of it!"

One short week later all of Canada, all of the United States, all of the world knew how to pronounce the name of the star of the 1976 Olympic Games—the name of Nadia Comăneci. And today the "Incredible Comaneech," as she is widely referred to, bears a name that will last forever in the annals of sport.

The difficulty in pronouncing Nadia's family name is due to most of the world's inability to read Romanian, especially the letters "ă" and "ci." But the prime reason for the mispronunciation was the total lack of familiarity with the gymnast's name despite the fact that, even before the Montreal Olympics, Nadia was a star of the gymnastic world.

In 1975, the thirteen-year-old Nadia Comaneci of Romania was crowned the European women's gymnastic queen, having captured four of five possible gold medals and, in so doing, defeating the world champion of women's gymnastics, Lyudmila Turishcheva of the Soviet Union.

Of course, any dedicated gymnastics fan knew all about Nadia, but to the world at large another name—that of the heroine of the Munich Olympic Games, Olga Korbut of the Soviet Union—was synonymous with gymnastic excellence. The darling pigtailed Olga had conquered the hearts of

Multiple exposure shows a succession of moves on the balance beam (*United Press International*)

everyone with her unprecedented feats and charming smile. Everybody was looking forward to seeing her and her teammates at Montreal.

When Nadia coolly stated before the Olympic Games that Olga would travel to Canada to smile, but that she would come to take the gold medals home to Romania, the press tended to regard her statement with some reservations. Russian gymnasts had proved for years and years that they were the "big names"—and Olga's reputation in competition was foremost in everyone's memory.

As for the name of Nadia Comaneci, it was little known. Few names from Romania made the sports pages. If any American had heard of Romania in connection with sports it was because of Ilie Nastase, often called "the nasty Romanian tennis player." So the declarations of the bold little

girl and her coaches were dismissed by the assembled world press with skeptical smiles. But many gymnastics experts quickly assessed why Nadia was so sure of herself, especially when they saw her performance at the "Gymnastics Demonstration" in Montreal on July 12-13 just prior to the quadrennial games.

ON JULY 18, 1976 in the huge Forum, best known to the sports world as an ice-hockey palace, the Olympic Team Classification Gymnastics Competition took place. It was the first time Nadia was seen by the world on TV. From that initial moment on the electronic screen, all cameras, all eyes and all attention were directed to one young gymnast dressed in white—the girl with the serious mien, Nadia Comaneci.

Her performance made many a heart almost come to a stop, or beat wildly in excitement as she competed, displaying her unique gymnastic talents. The audience responded to her efforts with thunderous applause each time she completed her performance. The electricity in the air of the huge St. Catherine Street arena seemed to play havoc with the electronic scoreboard. To everyone's amazement, the board indicated that one judge scored Nadia with a . . . 1.00! Even the sophisticated electronic apparatus, it seemed, was not ready for the Romanian's rhapsodic performance. Instead of showing the perfect "10.0" the judge had awarded her, the board spewed forth a surprising 1.00 to the dismay of everyone in the packed building—competitors, judges and audience alike.

From that moment on, the little girl from Onesti proved her total gymnastic supremacy. Her style denoted a new gymnastic school concept. The myth of Russian invincibility was destroyed. And after a few hurried conferences in broadcast booths, the name of Comaneci was irrevocably to be pronounced exactly as she herself pronounces it.

Sports commentators were soon to say that the referees gave Nadia's performance a perfect ten points because they had prematurely rushed to high scores for competitors who appeared earlier; and, of course, trying to respect the proportion of individual execution, they were then forced to score Nadia with the highest possible points. But in retrospect, even if Nadia had performed without any competition, she could have scored no less than perfect in most instances. That perfection had to be recorded because the young Romanian girl displayed, for the first time, a new art: the art of gymnastics, the art of acrobatic movement, the art of aerial ballet, the art of epitomizing what the human body can do in the form of gymnastics.

The Montreal Forum, used to world-class displays of hockey talent on ice, vibrated with the feeling that something unusual and important would happen that evening in the world of gymnastics.

Back home in Onesti
(*Bob Greene, New York*)

Everyone—the experts, the non-experts, the "enemies" of gymnastics—was fascinated by Nadia's performance. An intrigued world was glued to its TV sets, and sat transfixed by the small screens following the breath-taking performances in Canada's metropolis. It was late at night and the last report was over, but everybody was anxious to see Nadia at least one more time—at least a picture of her. The Canadian Broadcasting Corporation commentator was announcing an Olympics "promo": "Today you can see Nadia Comaneci again!" The world's major newspapers bore headlines with Nadia's name and front-page pictures of her. *Newsweek* portrayed her slender figure on its cover, proclaiming in bold type, "A star is born." Newsmen at radio stations everywhere in the world pronounced with accented perfection the Romanian name of the little girl with big, almond-shaped eyes.

Her fame spread with the bursting morning dawn carrying with it the legend, the mystery, that was Nadia. A daughter of Romania, now she belonged to the world.

WHENCE CAME THIS GIRL?

What did she do to be hailed the "Princess of the Olympic Games"?

Who is Nadia Comaneci?

What is her secret?

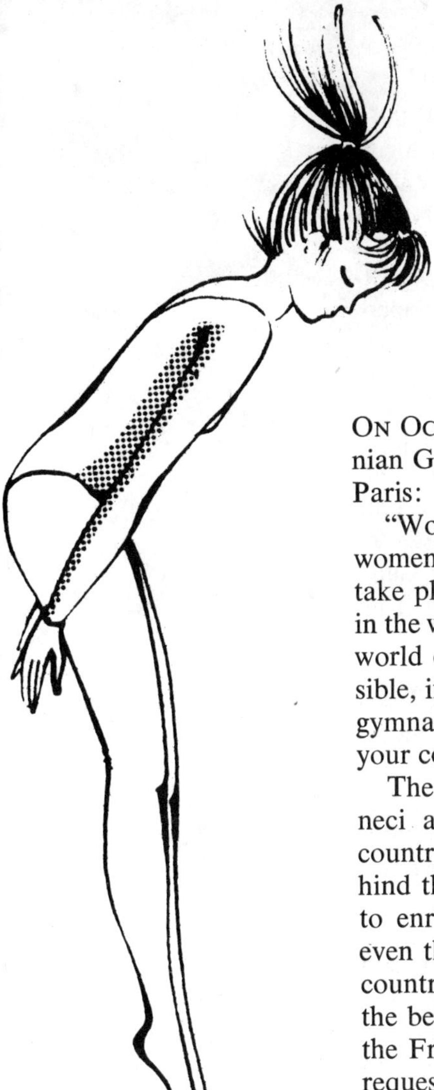

1

Tsukahara's Vault

On October 26, 1974, an official of the Romanian Gymnastics Federation received a call from Paris:

"Would you honor us please by sending two women gymnasts for a big exhibition which will take place in Paris. We expect the best gymnasts in the world, including Lyudmila Turishcheva, the world champion. We would appreciate it, if possible, if you sent the champion Romanian woman gymnast and the second best woman gymnast of your country." The invitation was accepted.

The Federation decided to send Nadia Comaneci and Teodora Ungureanu rather than the country's champion, Alina Goreac. The reason behind this decision was to allow the younger girls to enrich their competitive experience. In fact, even though Nadia was not the champion of her country at that time, she was considered by many the best woman gymnast of Romania. Therefore, the French audience would have the best—their request would be completely satisfied.

The gymnasts were to leave in three days; formalities revolving around passports and visas accelerated to breakneck speeds. And, like all mothers, Nadia's mother was determined that everything would be ready—and right. She washed and ironed clothing and gymsuits for the trip. She also baked the cakes that Nadia is fond of. And Nadia's father helped too—he worried!

The flight was bumpy but, exhausted by the preparations, Nadia and Teodora slept on the plane. Their coach, Bela Karoli, who told the story of their trip in the Romanian magazine, *Sport,* was thankful for their calm.

Finally the plane landed at Le Bourget airport. The corridors of the terminal were crowded, as usual, and the two little girls clung to Bela's hands. Anxious and anticipatory, the trio found nobody waiting for them. After half an hour the coach donned his jacket, on the back of which was printed in large letters, "ROMANIA." That, he hoped, would draw attention to their presence—if, indeed, anyone was there to meet them.

An hour passed until, finally, a little old man limped up to them, identifying himself as their translator. Into a cab they went and, after an adventurous trip, they arrived at the Ile des Vents hall where the exhibition was to be held that very day. The translator disappeared and the Romanian coach and his two charges were prevented from entering the hall.

Vainly the coach tried to explain to the ticket-takers about the invitation. The employees knew a women's gymnastics performance was going on inside, but they felt neither the huge Romanian nor the two little girls he had with him seemed to belong. After a long discussion—handicapped without the translator—Bela Karoli succeeded in getting inside the gymnastics hall, leaving the two tired girls sitting on their suitcases outside.

After a frustrating few minutes, Bela found the translator who told him the Romanian girls were scheduled to perform in the gymnasium of a private school. A van was to take them, along with the Polish and Bulgarian women gymnastics, to the school building. Bela Karoli was speechless. He realized the confusion; the French officials were expecting Alina Goreac, the Romanian champion. Nobody in Bucharest had bothered to announce the change in the cast of characters. Nadia's and Teodora's names meant nothing to the officials at Ile des Vents where the great Russian champion Lyudmila Turishcheva was to perform.

It took an hour and a half for the little van to make the trip across Paris to the school. The girls took a few minutes to dress for the microexhibition, and then stepped inside the gymnasium. The view that greeted them was more than depressing:

Karoli wraps Nadia's elbow as an extra precaution
(*Bruce Curtis*)

a cement floor spotted with a few mats. Added to that, they saw perhaps thirty to forty spectators who seemed to be students at the school, but who were smoking and walking freely around the gymnastic equipment.

The Polish and Bulgarian women gymnasts refused to perform, and with good reason: the cement floor was a great danger. Only Nadia and Teodora started their warm-up. Soon, embarrassed by the seriousness of the two little girls, the audience took their seats and stubbed out their cigarettes.

The exhibition began. The audience kept a respectful silence—studiously impressed by the unbelievable skill of the two children. After each event, the crowd burst into wild applause and called for encores. Pleased by the turn of events, the Romanian girls satisfied their small audience and the cheering seemed to go on forever.

Meanwhile, Bela Karoli was worried about the time. It was 6:30 and the main exhibition at the big Ile des Vents hall had started; there was no time to waste. Nadia and Teodora put their long coats on over their gymnastics suits, ran out and found, to their dismay, that the van had left. Fortunately, the disappearing translator was still there, but he knew nothing about the van.

There was a hotel near the school. Pulling the limping old man after him, Bela tried to determine if there was a car there. The clerk knew nothing, could not do anything, and didn't want to interfere with anything.

Karoli, trying to be as resourceful as possible, asked the translator to call a taxi, agreeing to pay for it himself. Suddenly the translator became helpful. In fifteen minutes a taxicab arrived, but the driver was skeptical about making it to the big hall in less than two hours. With professional disdain he reminded them it was rush hour in Paris.

During the whole trip Bela Karoli saw red before his eyes—maybe because the taxicab seemed to catch every red light. He shook the translator, urging him to rush the driver. But there was nothing to be done.

At 8:35 P.M., the translator pointed toward a lighted tower: "There's Ile des Vents." Five minutes later, Karoli jumped from the taxi, pulling his girls after him, asking the translator to leave all the luggage in the corridors without taking any responsibility. But once again, at the entrance, the coach and his two charges were stopped by ticket-takers and the same senseless discussion was repeated in two languages. Angry over the multiplicity of misunderstandings, Karoli made a decision: putting an arm around each girl's shoulders, he suddenly leaned forward and took off, breaking the wall of stubborn, uniformed employees, running straight to the exhibition hall and breathlessly hiding the three of them behind a pile of mats. Suddenly they heard an announcement: "Now vaulting: Lyudmila Turishcheva!"

Leaving the girls behind the pile of mats, Karoli ran toward the officials. Out of nowhere (Karoli still can't explain it) appeared the old little man, limping along behind him. They started to explain the situation, seeking to correct the mistake. But an official said coldly, in an infuriating Gallic manner as he looked at his desk: "The forms don't say anything!"

Bela was seething so, he almost stepped on the line along which Miss Turishcheva was going to run preparatory to her jump. Three men dragged him away, forcing him to lie on the ground in order to give the audience good visibility. An electrifying silence filled the elegant gymnasium; Turishcheva was ready to vault. She started her approach, but the Romanian coach didn't see anything. His brain was racing to find a solution, a decision, a way out of this dilemma. He was brought back to reality by the applause and cheers: "Tu-ri-shche-va! Tu-ri-shche-va!"

Taking advantage of the uproar, the coach signaled Nadia. Removing her overcoat, the little girl came out from behind the mats, ran toward the vault start, and took the initial position. Nobody paid any attention to the child. Suddenly, Karoli was hit with a painful thought: Nadia didn't know

that horse vault, she didn't have her own mark on the carpet, she never had vaulted in that gymnasium. But she was already looking straight ahead at the horse and was awaiting her coach's signal. The Romanian coach stepped forward and raised his arms in the international signal for silence.

The audience, which had not yet spotted Nadia, was slowly becoming quieter, staring in surprise at the man with his upraised arms. In a few seconds, when the noise abated, Karoli gave Nadia the start signal. As she started to run, Karoli dropped to the floor again. Nadia was moving faster and faster toward the springboard. He heard its "sproing" as

Nadia took off. Flying through the air, she performed the difficult "Tsukahara" jump over an unknown vault horse, knowing not what was behind it, landing mat or dark abyss.

Tsukahara's vault

The springboard's reverberations echoed in the deep silence, and Nadia's best "Tsukahara" was completed with a perfect landing, as she froze like an unmoving bronze statue. In a fraction of a moment, the audience reacted ecstatically. The ovation exceeded anything Bela Karoli ever heard.

Turishcheva, who was exchanging smiling greetings with the audience on the opposite side of the carpet, turned her head, amazed by the new outburst of enthusiasm. Instinctively, she realized what was happening.

Lonely little Nadia returned to the starting line, not knowing how to react to the huge, warm ovation. The audience started to shout at the announcer seeking the gymnast's name. The puzzled announcer sought help with his eyes from the officials. The officials looked at each other with unmasked astonishment.

Karoli ran to the translator and pushed him to the microphone. There followed the strangest presentation of a champion. The rambling words were without logic, almost without meaning to the audience.

"A Romanian woman gymnast vaulted Tsukahara . . . She is not Romania's champion . . . Please, forgive us because she doesn't appear on the program . . . She is thirteen years old. . . ."

The translator pushed the announcer away and started to shout into the microphone, giving details about Nadia's life, information he had learned from Bela Karoli during the nightmarish trips in the van and taxicab. The audience's excitement reached a noisy buzz when Nadia's age was mentioned.

Little by little, the arena calmed down. Turishcheva demanded of the jury why her vault had not been the last as the schedule called for. The members of the jury could give no answer, but they promised to find out.

Meanwhile, Nadia started to warm up even though she didn't know whether she would perform or not. An official charged out at the Romanian coach and an angry conversation ensued—with the little old translator in the middle, trying to clear up the contretemps for both sides. The French official screamed about respecting the program; the Romanian coach, about his 3,000-kilometer trip. When the uneven parallel bars were free, Bela again signaled with his hands and Nadia dove toward them. Her movement was so unexpected that all the gymnasts stopped what they were doing and watched Nadia's execution. The audience was arrested into total silence until Nadia completed her dismount, again landing on she-knew-not-

A perfect jump, the fingers of each hand as symmetrical as the point of each toe
(*Bruce Curtis*)

what. Then the crowd started to cheer and clap more wildly than before.

Teodora and Nadia synchronize a dance
(*Bob Greene, New York*)

Nadia disappeared behind the pile of mats. Now her coach had to tell her that the organizers of the exhibition couldn't allow any more "illegal" performances. Nadia listened calmly, continuing her warm-up; Teodora watched silently, not understanding what was going on.

On the balance beam, Turishcheva started her exercises, sure of herself, showing tremendous skill and pride. Her routine was great and her landing was perfect. But the audience didn't have a chance to reward the great Russian champion with plaudits, because the Romanian coach screamed to Nadia, "Go, now!"—and Nadia jumped on the beam without a wasted moment.

Thus the Parisian audience had the unique opportunity of seeing the greatest performance of their lives. Nadia left imagination behind, while her coach prayed that nothing untoward would happen to her.

But something did happen: for the third time, a hurricane of applause swept through the gymnasium. Nadia had made a perfect landing after a spectacular dismount. The ovation seemed endless.

Regardless, the Romanian coach waited with great anxiety, fearing some dreadful official action. But, on the contrary, the French officials started to smile at the Romanians, and Bela realized intuitively that both Nadia and Teodora would be allowed to perform in the evening's last event, the floor exercises.

The audience didn't let up its cheering and applause for one second, encouraging Nadia to partake in the floor event. But again the jinx of the trip showed its unlucky face to the three Romanians. The music tapes for the floor program were in the suitcases and their luggage was far off at some other place in the building. Bela looked for the translator again. But the little old limping man had disappeared one more time; he was, they discovered later, giving "interviews" to curious questioners. Bela considered for a fleeting second asking the French pianist to play for Nadia, but he realized there was no way to synchronize the music with the motion of Nadia's floor exercises. And the audience was waiting.

The coach looked at his charges as if waiting for an answer. The girls were silent. Nadia, not knowing what to do, looked up at the elegant ceiling. Following her eyes up to the dome of the hall, Bela suddenly had an idea. It would be unusual for a floor exercise, but it seemed the only way to save the situation. He walked over to the girls, knelt to be at the same level, and whispered in their ears.

After a few moments, the girls started their floor event, executing movements together as if one were the mirror reflection of the other. Like movie trick photography, they moved apart and met again, with mathematical precision, at great speed, in perfect rhythm.

The audience was on its feet before the end of the floor exercises. The depth and warmth of the applause rewarded the small Romanian team, affording it remarkable recognition of an unforgettable performance, of unbelievable courage, self-denial and boldness, and a love of gymnastics.

Bela Karoli wiped a tear from his cheek; not only because of the French audience's appreciation, but because of Nadia's victory, won by her own skills when she started to run toward the vaulting horse, doing one of the most difficult gymnastic exercises, "Tsukahara's" vault—an exercise for *men*!

She had overcome a major challenge, one which showed her talent and her determined ambition to do what she knew had to be done. Maybe one gymnast in thousands would have dared to start a run such as that without a warm-up, following a great gymnast like Lyudmila Turishcheva. Maybe no other gymnast in the world would! But nothing was as hard as to make Nadia or her coach back away from their aim—and nothing would stop them in the future.

On that evening in Paris, Nadia won, in effect, the European title—won it seven months before the European championship took place!

2

"Who Likes Gymnastics?"

ONESTI[1] IS SITUATED in Moldavia, an historic province in the eastern part of Romania, 300 kilometers (about 185 miles) from Bucharest. Its population is about sixty thousand. It bears the look of any typical workers' city—street after street of row houses and no outstanding architecture. Onesti is, in fact, one of the country's most industrialized cities and that explains why the majority of the population is quite young.

Children, obviously, are an extremely important part of the population and the regime is conscious of the need to take good care of them. Sports and other recreational activities for children of all ages are heavily subsidized by the government. As part of his job, Bela Karoli, a gymnastics coach, regularly scouted for potential new gymnasts in the kindergartens of the city.

It was the recess period and the jostling, noisy children in the schoolyard were crowded together. Karoli suddenly noticed two little girls playing at a gymnastics routine, doing a lot of jumping and graceful ballet steps with remarkable imagination.

He looked on, amazed, for a while and then decided to speak to the girls. As he made his way among the cheerfully loud groups of children, the school bell sounded, marking the end of recess. The coach unhappily lost sight of the girls as they rushed into the school with the other children.

He sought, and got, permission to look for them, going from classroom to classroom, in the hope of recognizing them—but he couldn't spot them.

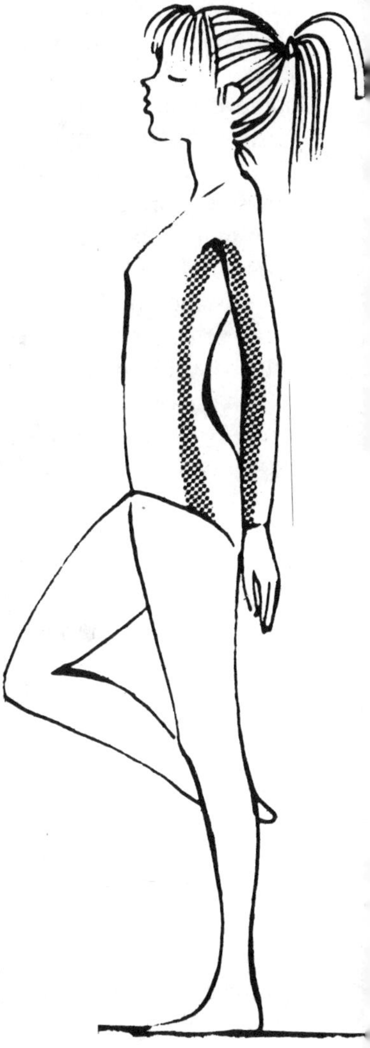

[1] The city is now known officially as Gheorghe-Gheorghiu-Dej by the name of the first Communist president of Romania; everyone, however, still calls it by its old name, Onesti.

When he completed his first search, Karoli asked permission of the school authorities to make a second attempt to find the girls. Slowly and carefully he started once again to go from classroom to classroom, scanning each child with his eyes, but again the search ended with the same result: he was unable to recognize the two girls.

There was nothing for the coach to do but leave. But a strong intuitive sense told him to try still a third time. Almost feeling foolish, he asked permission again to try to find the children whose antics in the schoolyard had attracted his attention. So, for the third time, he started to walk through the classrooms. This time however, he changed his tactics. In each room he asked the same question: "Who likes gymnastics?" In one classroom, two little girls jumped to their feet. One of them was called Nadia. Her full name: Nadia Comaneci!

When Bela Karoli asked Nadia's parents if they would agree to have Nadia take gymnastics lessons, her mother was more than relieved. In three years, she indicated later, Nadia had broken four sofas by jumping on the springs.

When Karoli began to give her lessons, Nadia was six years old. She was born in Onesti on November 12, 1961, the first-born child of Stefania-Alexandrina and Gheorghe Comaneci. Gheorghe chose her name in memory of a pleasant evening spent at the movies with his wife, then pregnant with Nadia. Stefania first felt her baby kick during a film that had as its heroine a woman named Nadia. The Comaneci family is typical of working-class families in many parts of the world. Both parents work to earn enough to provide comforts for Nadia and her younger brother, Adrian. The father is an automotive mechanic, the mother an office worker.

This background was, perhaps, Nadia's good fortune. She didn't come from an intellectual family with grandiose plans for their children's futures. Nadia, of course, immensely enjoyed her gymnastics training because of her innate talent.

But, thankfully, she was not pushed into taking piano or French lessons as are many other offspring born into more sophisticated families. In addition, Nadia's family never prevented her from practicing hour upon hour, six days a week. To the contrary, Nadia's parents cooperated with Bela Karoli and trusted him implicitly, as their simple and healthy instincts directed them. Actually, Bela offered a major advantage as a coach: he was married. His wife, Marta, was all the assurance the parents needed that the little gymnasts would be carefully supervised and kindly treated. And Nadia's parents, as well as many others like them, were right. Marta and Bela Karoli proved through the years that they were like second parents to all their little gymnastic girls.

Nadia with her mother and brother Adrian
(*Wide World Photos*)

Marta and Bela Karoli were a young married couple when, in 1968, they decided to open a small children's gymnastics class. Actually, they had been scouting for young talented girls in gymnastics for the previous five years.

Marta was a gymnast. Bela, on the other hand, had had next to nothing in common with gymnastics. But, as he recognized later, when he fell in love with Marta, he fell in love with gymnastics too.

About the same time that Nadia was discovered by Bela, the Karolis had decided to work with a group of twenty-six young girls to develop them as gymnasts, despite the long-held theory that gymnastics should be embarked upon only after a boy or girl had passed puberty. Marta and Bela assumed the "risk" of starting their girls much earlier.

According to accepted theory, after pubescence children are likely to grow quite tall or heavy. Their ability to perform gymnastics might be much poorer than before, and all the hard work would be wasted. Obviously, Marta and Bela Karoli knew how to select future women gymnasts they wished to coach: they looked for girls with long legs, small joints, delicate figures and small hips, girls who were good at running and jumping, girls with exceptional coordination and a desire to do hard work.

It is of interest to relate the test used to select the Karoli protégées. Marta and Bela employed as an "admission" exam three events: a 15-meter sprint, a long jump, and a walk on the balance beam. While the first two events were important, the last one was decisive. If a girl was afraid on the beam, she was immediately disqualified as a pupil .The Karolis also sought only girls who they felt had native intelligence: children with quick eyes and a demeanor that bespoke an abundance of "life energy."

Marta and Bela Karoli, husband-and-wife coaching team
(*Bob Greene, New York*)

Nadia drew all eyes from the very beginning due to her exceptional gymnastic talents. That talent made her coaches determined to teach her more and more of the elements of gymnastics, as well as to make the other girls keep up with Nadia; in brief, to accelerate the whole gymnastic routine for beginners.

As TIME PROVED, Karoli was an energetic and bold coach. He utilized his wife's gymnastic knowledge and applied it with an innate power of anticipation. He had actually had basic training in gymnastics at the Institute of Physical Education and Sports in Bucharest from which he and his wife graduated in 1963. But he started over again at "point zero" as a coach. He learned with his charges everything from the basic "attention position." He was not hampered by previously learned standard gymnastics routines, inasmuch as he had never been taught them himself. He allowed his pupils to express their talents which proved, in most cases, to produce greater achievements than any traditional scholastic routine.

Everybody knows that great champions never make good coaches. This is a truism. Former champions have too much ego; their personalities are too dominant to allow any other personality and talent to develop near them. Bela "grew up" with his little girls, time and again defying the long-accepted rules of teaching, for the simple reason that, at a six-year-old level, there aren't many rules.

Marta, by contrast, was a conservative type of coach, supervising the correcting of mistakes, trying to understand failures and—more than anything else—teaching the little girls the grace of movement, the art of motion and the beauty of dance in each of the rhythmic patterns.

From the very beginning, Nadia was taught to be sure of herself, to trust her coaches and to work hard. It is no secret that children have more energy and can work harder than adults. But Nadia's work capacity surpassed anyone's imagination. She could do the same motion scores of times in

Handstand in the split position—on a four-inch base
(*Joe DiMaggio*)

Karoli catches Nadia in mid-flight
(*Bob Greene, New York*)

a row without rest. She could spin around bars over and over again, doing painful routines without complaint. She could practice hours on end without sign of fatigue. Her body adapted itself to hard work and "taught" her how to work with minimum effort but maximum efficiency.

On the other hand, Nadia had that uniquely rare quality of understanding any explanation in seconds, materializing it quickly into perfect execution. Her native talent for learning speedily and her strong will enabled her two coaches to teach her more and more new elements and combinations in gymnastics.

At the same time, Nadia was daily doing ballet and leg- and arm-spring exercises. Ballet was necessary for improving her elegance of movement and expressiveness. The "spring" exercises were to develop both leg and arm muscles so that they could be used to push off fast, high and easily.

Encouraged by her successes, Nadia developed another of her native qualities: courage. Even her coaches were amazed by her courage. Nadia was able and prepared to work without assistance from the very beginning—unless there was actual chance of danger. Years later when he was asked if Nadia had ever shown fear, or if she had ever cried, her coach answered without a moment's hesitation with a simple "No."

Most of the time, Bela watched Nadia from a distance, concerned more with the perfection and expressivity of her work than with helping her. Bela helped Nadia more often when she was doing vaulting exercises. Here there was a sizable advantage due to his huge figure and his strength. Many times, he stopped Nadia in mid-flight eight or nine feet off the ground.

In the beginning a great deal of the time was spent helping the girls adapt to the gymnastics apparatus. Marta and Bela knew how to make the children trust the apparatus, to approach it in a friendly manner, to feel comfortable on it, to do the thousands of exercises enabling them to gain the feeling of the "machinery" of the gymnasium.

Nadia's precision and amazing balance came from that very early training period when she "played" with the gymnastics equipment. She learned to keep it under her total control and command—not the reverse. In gymnastics, more than in any other sport, fear is the most negative factor for a competitor.

Her schedule was crowded from the beginning. She couldn't complete a daily workout in less than four hours. She worked in the gymnastics classroom six days a week. She never tried to skip a lesson. She always was the first to start the warm-

Nadia cools her hand for a better grip on the bar
(*Bob Greene, New York*)

up exercises. Her devotion to her work was beyond belief.

From that great devotion came her serious attitude toward gymnastics. Of course, she knew how to laugh, smile and play like any child her age. But her training was a continuous concentration of work, a continuous search for new ways to reach perfection—and she learned it all from her coaches.

From the beginning one thing was very clear for each child in the Karoli class: "Gymnastics means, first of all, hard work; it means serious work. Otherwise, dangerous consequences can occur."

NADIA'S GYMNASTICS EDUCATION was so strict and firm that even after she became a star, she couldn't manage to behave other than the way she was used to. In Romania, speaking about success in sports, people say, "The coach is everything." In Nadia's case the proverb applied perfectly, especially regarding her attitude toward gymnastics.

But sometimes "the army makes a brave general," and this is also true of Nadia's coaches. Bela Karoli himself, speaking of Nadia's beginnings, said, "I saw nothing fantastic in her on the first day. . . . But in a short time, Nadia Comaneci distinguished herself through particular aptitudes: mobility, suppleness, speed of response, ability to learn difficult executions, desire to work and to learn as much as possible in gymnastics."

Surely any coach would be happy to have six-year-old Nadia to work with. But that doesn't mean Marta's and Bela's merits are to be belittled! Perhaps many a coach could have taught Nadia as many elements of gymnastics, but how many could have taught her to compete as she does? A whole book could be written about Nadia's ability to compete, about her self-determination, about her desire to win. If all her physical, mental, esthetic and moral qualities are her own innate heritage, the ability to compete is surely the Karolis' gift to her. Nadia was entered in local competitions from the very beginning in order to develop her ambition, her competitiveness, and her self-control. Moreover, Bela knew (or perhaps his intuitions told him) one benefit about an early start in competition: by competing at so young an age, Nadia would become used to the mental stress of performing in front of audiences and judges, and would quickly adapt herself to competitive conditions. She competed so many times that competition eventually become a natural occurrence.

Her coaches taught her how to control her emotions, her nervousness and her worries; taught her how to concentrate on her performance and on nothing else. She was taught to be serious and calm when, in fact, her first impulses were no different than anyone else's—to be nervous and try to have a little fun. She grew up in competitive situations much as a professor's child grows up in the middle of academia.

Only a year after she saw a gymnastics hall for the first time, Nadia was the youngest competitor in the Romanian National Junior Championships. She finished in thirteenth place. The following year, she won the same competition—at the tender age of eight! Now, after the Olympic Games, she is fifteen years old and has won almost all twenty of the international gymnastics competitions she has entered.

In previous times, a girl only started to learn the first steps of gymnastics at the age of fifteen. At that tender age, Nadia Comaneci is the youngest European champion, and the youngest Olympic champion in gymnastics. She has defeated all the women gymnastic stars of her time.

At fifteen, her name is already a legend because she was not afraid to stand up when an intelligent and brave coach asked, "Who likes gymnastics?"

3

A Day in the Life

THE COMANECI FAMILY used to live on Onesti street, but now that Nadia has become a gymnastic star they live right near Nadia's school, in a ten-story building with modern facilities. They are now also close to Onesti's modern gymnastics hall. Significantly, the name of the street on which they now live translates to "The Youth" Street.

In the family apartment, Nadia's presence is everywhere. On shelves in most of the rooms are dolls of different sizes and "nationalities" from more than sixty countries. Her biggest doll, named Fragolina, usually sits on a sofa.

The apartment is furnished with new furniture called "Bacau" (which happens to be the name of the county in which the city of Onesti is located); furniture covered with beautiful white embroidery. Through the glass of a sideboard door, one can see shelves teeming with trophies, skillfully arranged according to size. On the TV set (a Russian-built "Cosmos 3") is a red crystal cup, "The Cup of Europe" which she won in Norway in 1975. Also to be seen is an "Honored Master of Sports" diploma, the highest distinction accorded by the Romanian government in the sports field. Half of one wall is covered by an almost-life-size photograph of Nadia working on the balance beam—a poster made by Tony Duffy. To the left of the poster is a photograph of Nadia taken on her first day in grammar school: she is wearing her hair in braids with a big red bow. To the right of the poster is a photo of her younger brother Adrian, also taken on his first day of school. Above the telephone table is another photo of Nadia, her hair combed in two braids as in the earlier picture.

Adrian is ten but he doesn't indulge in gymnastics. Occasionally, when Nadia has free time, she makes him do many of the kinds of jumps and even tries to teach him to "split forward," which doesn't work out too well. Adrian would rather do weightlifting. As far as he is concerned, lifting weights is "the real thing," a man's sport. Unfortunately he is not permitted to partake in sports for reasons of health. Like everybody around the house, Adrian is a great admirer of Nadia's successes—and he is the first judge of her performance.

Nadia's parents are, obviously, her biggest fans in the world. And, of course, they are the ones

A leap from a playground swing as Teodora looks on (*Bob Greene, New York*)

who worry most about Nadia's future, and each of her future trips abroad.

NADIA IS A CHILD, but a very unusual one—she is far too serious. Yet her attitude is to be expected. Anybody who works that hard will naturally become serious. Nadia speaks little, especially when she is being interviewed, because she doesn't know exactly how to deal with all her growing glory—and she prefers to be modest. Her modesty surprises everyone, even her mother.

That doesn't mean Nadia hasn't any pride. Her pride is great and she uses it when she trains, when she studies for school and, most of all, when she competes. In fact, her life is the product of her pride, her ambition, and her personality.

Her life belongs to a gymnastics career, but Nadia also has a private life, like any girl of fourteen or fifteen. She likes to read and to see movies, and she loves to play with her dolls.

Her doll collection has become quite famous. She has almost two hundred dolls from all over the world. Her passion for dolls developed along with her gymnastics skills.

In 1970, when Nadia competed in the Romanian National Junior Championships, she was, as already noted, the youngest competitor, and she finished in thirteenth place. Because the number thirteen was considered unlucky by Nadia's coach, Bela Karoli countered one superstition with another: he gave her an Eskimo doll to ward off the evil number. He also advised her never to rank that low in competition again. Nadia carried her lucky doll everywhere she went after that. Whether or not the doll and advice had anything to do with it, she won the event at the championships the next year. Or could it have been because she was older?

Nadia's movie idol, Alain Delon, French film star (*Unifrance*)

Soccer is Nadia's favorite recreation
(*Bob Greene, New York*)

In any case, she now buys dolls from every place she competes, each doll having a special meaning for her. The doll she bought in Montreal, for example, is a constant reminder of her first 10 in the Olympics! Any gymnast in the world would be happy to have a doll—if he or she could be assured of a 10. And a collection of two hundred dolls . . . ?

She also has an idol. Not a gymnast nor a sports figure. Her idol is the French movie star, Alain Delon.

BEFORE SHE BEGAN gymnastics lessons, Nadia was somewhat of a "problem child." Her mother recalls that the young girl was always "full of life." So full of life was she, in fact, that her parents often used to get complaints from the parents of *boys* about her aggressiveness, about fighting with them—because she enjoyed playing with boys especially. She was usually the "troublemaker" in her group and her parents were forced to keep her inside the house many times as punishment for her fights.

But it was a greater problem keeping Nadia in the house; she couldn't stay still for a second. The sofas were her victims. Bela Karoli couldn't have found a better moment to ask Nadia's parents if their daughter could practice gymnastics.

Nadia still loves boys' games. She adores playing soccer with the boys in front of her apartment building or in the courtyard. Most of the time, Nadia plays with her best friend, Teodora Ungureanu, against Adrian and his friend. It is not very hard to figure out which team is usually the winner. She also likes to swim, to bicycle and ski, but all these when she is not occupied in training for an important competition. During the training period, she relaxes from the acrobatic and risky gymnastics exercises by playing badminton.

Nadia is currently an eighth-grade student at the Sports High School. Each morning, six days a week, she attends classes from eight o'clock to noon or, sometimes, until one o'clock. Nadia is a conscientious and good student. She feels most at ease with her studies in chemistry, French and English, but she has excellent marks in all school subjects—without special attention from the teaching faculty. Her course average is above 9 points[1] and she does her homework with the same seriousness as she approaches gymnastics.

WHEN NADIA was an infant, when she was a preschooler, even when she started to practice gymnastics, her mother did not prepare any special type of meal for her, simply because nobody knew anything about her gymnastic talents. Therefore Nadia ate what her family ate, and that diet would make most North American calorie-conscious families gasp. Romanian food! Romanians serve almost everything they cook with heavy gravies and greasy, roasted flour. The national dish is pork-stuffed cabbage, with cornmeal mush.

[1] In the Romanian teaching system, marks range from 1 to 10, rather than to 100 as in the North American systems.

The prosperity of a Romanian family is most often judged by the number of meat meals served in one day and the abundance of sweet desserts on the table. "Sugar-free" foods or "low calorie" meals are practically unknown in Romania. Every family's ambition is to raise a pig to kill for Christmas, preserving the uneaten pork in the animal's own melted fat in order to keep it for the rest of the year.

Nadia ate what her parents ate, hearty Romanian food. The diet of special vegetable salads North American reporters saw her eating was the special food regimen required before a gymnastics competition. A stomach full of heavy food takes a lot of energy to digest, disturbs a restful sleep and makes a gymnast "heavier" in her executions. The same reporters were surprised, however, to see Nadia's coach hand her bread and sugar in sizable quantities.

Enjoying a class at school
(Bob Greene, New York)

Her regular diet is, in fact, a good healthy natural meal. Her mother knows how to cook in the old-fashioned Romanian tradition. Each time Nadia leaves for a competition, her mother bakes a lot of cakes for Nadia to take with her. And none of the cakes contains sugar substitutes. Nadia's beautiful figure is shaped by the tremendous amounts of energy expended during her four to six hours of daily workouts, and not by a special sophisticated diet.

After a work-out
(*Bob Greene, New York*)

Nadia and her teammates don't go to school by bus, don't go shopping sitting in a car, and don't sit half the day in front of a TV set. Nadia works all day long. However, her mother knows how to feed the child without using any secret or miraculous diet recipes.

NADIA LIVES an active sports life. Her daily schedule is crowded. Usually, she finishes classes at noon. In the afternoon she naps for two and a half hours; then she works out at the gym between 5:00 and 8:00 in the evening—sometimes even longer. She also reserves a few hours for school homework.

Her school vacations are usually filled with competitions. When she rests, she goes to a little resort town in the beautiful Moldavian mountains. But she spends most of her vacations living in sports camps, training hard. Before major competitions, Nadia and her teammates live in a special park reservation in Bucharest, a sports complex called "23 AUGUST." It is the central sports headquarters, the heart of Romania's sports activities. Here she is exposed to the best coaches, the best specialists, the best physicians, the best conditions, and the best care granted to Romania's sports elite. At this camp, Nadia follows a strict schedule, everything being arranged to help her achieve the best form before any important competition. She works under the same conditions as she would in competition, doing each exercise over and over hundreds of times. Every detail is supervised and polished, and Nadia has nothing to worry about except her gymnastic routine.

Three daily meals are cooked in the Romanian manner, but are enriched with a lot of vegetables and fresh fruit desserts. Two snacks are also served daily, consisting of chocolate, oranges and other fruits, or dried cakes.

At camp, Nadia and her teammates take a long nap in the afternoon and get sleep nightly between 10:30 P.M. and 7:30 A.M. She sleeps in a big dormitory with the others in Bela Karoli's gymnastic team. She has never had any problem falling asleep, an important factor in considering Nadia's general strength. The gymnastics practice hours at camp are usually between 8:00 A.M. and 11:00 A.M., and then again between 5:00 P.M. and 8:00 P.M. or even later. Nadia works very hard during those hours, but she never seems to be really tired.

NADIA LOVES GYMNASTICS and she is very determined about her performances. She also loves her

Karoli has a few words with some of his gymnasts
(Bob Greene, New York)

dolls, and everybody seems to love her. She is a good comrade to her teammates, and her best friend continues to be her famous international gymnast teammate, Teodora Ungureanu. They are together all the time, even when they are not in camp.

Actually, Bela Karoli's gymnastic team is much like a family. He and his wife Marta are truly like the team's parents. They pay the same amount of attention to everybody and Nadia doesn't derive any benefit from special favors.

Because each girl in the team is equally important, each deserves and gets the same respect. Each deserves and gets the same time and energy from their coaches. Although each girl may answer to a different name—Nadia Comaneci, Teodora Ungureanu, Georgeta Gabor, Luminita Milea, Iuliana Marcu, Marilena Neacsu—each stood up when a Romanian coach asked the same question: "Who likes gymnastics?"

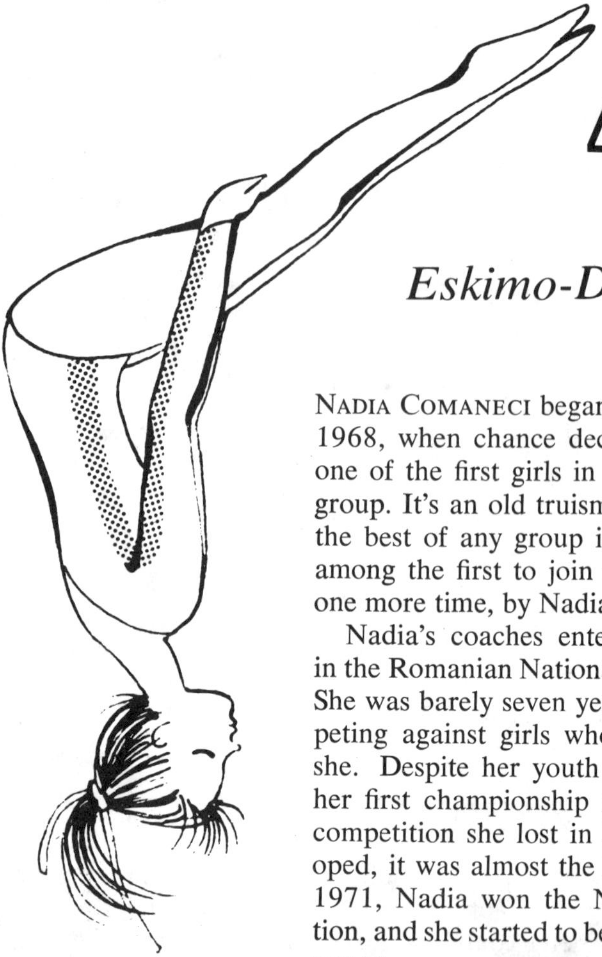

4

Eskimo-Doll Power

NADIA COMANECI began practicing gymnastics in 1968, when chance decreed she was to become one of the first girls in Bela and Marta Karoli's group. It's an old truism in the sports world that the best of any group is usually the one who is among the first to join it. That rule was proved one more time, by Nadia.

Nadia's coaches entered her two years later in the Romanian National Junior Championships. She was barely seven years old and she was competing against girls who were much older than she. Despite her youth she placed thirteenth in her first championship meet. That was the first competition she lost in her career and, it developed, it was almost the last! The following year, 1971, Nadia won the National Junior competition, and she started to believe in her Eskimo doll's power.

From that day on, the Eskimo doll would be Nadia's constant companion, present through the years every time Nadia competed. He would never disappoint her, never fail her trust in his power.

Her third year as a gymnast marked Nadia's selection to the Romanian girls gymnastics team and, for the first time, she competed in an international competition in 1971. It was a great honor for Nadia to don the gymnastics team uniform with the red, yellow and blue Romanian colors. As a proud member of Romania's junior team she went to Poland to compete against the Polish team in an inter-country match. Despite the fact she had no international competition under her belt, she took the first place in the all-round competition.

Extension preparatory to another back flip
(*Bruce Curtis*)

The Karolis' gymnastics class in the new sports center in Onesti
(*Bob Greene, New York*)

Then she went to Bulgaria to take part in the highly competitive international competition, the "Friendship Cup," the traditional annual competition among gymnasts of all the Communist countries. Despite all this high-calibered talent, she won the gold medals in two events; the uneven parallel bars and the balance beam. Nadia had begun to justify her coaches' expectations!

In the following year Nadia did not compete in any important gymnastics competitions. Nineteen hundred seventy-two was to be the crucial year of her career; the year when her coaches began to seek a new style for Nadia. They now knew she could win in an international competition, but they recognized that she must improve her routines with original and more difficult exercises. Her extraordinary talents demanded new forms of gymnastic executions, new expression of movements—in short, a personal style. That was the crucial moment, the day when the old traditional routines were discarded in favor of young, full-of-life, acrobatic, highly spectacular, new Romanian routines.

Step by step, Nadia and her coaches uncovered new possibilities, new combinations for her routines. An incredible amount of work was required of the ten-year-old gymnast and her coaches. It involved thousands of repetitive movements in order to polish one execution. It meant spending six hours daily in the gymnasium. It meant tremendous enthusiasm and boundless optimism on the part of Nadia and her coaches.

A strong relationship of mutual respect was cemented between Nadia and the Karolis. All this, because they had the same aims: to prove to the world their talent and to succeed in their ambition to win. On her eleventh birthday Nadia won the Romanian National Junior Championships.

Nadia was eleven and a half years old when she first took part in Romania's International Championships, a competition best known for the performances displayed by the leading women gymnasts both from Romania and abroad. She won five events! That surprised everybody, but it was nothing compared to the surprise that followed later in 1973. Competing in East Germany Nadia again won the traditional Friendship Cup, taking first place in the all-round competition and the uneven parallel bars and jumps, defeating the best gymnasts; among them, Nelli Kim of the U.S.S.R. and Anelore Zinke of East Germany. This triumph was, in fact, Nadia's first big international coup!

But Nadia was not the only product of Marta and Bela Karoli's efforts in gymnastics. From the first group of twenty-six young girls, many made names for themselves—and the Karolis—in Romanian gymnastics. One of them was Teodora Ungureanu who came in fourth to Nadia in the all-round event of the 1973 Friendship Cup competition in East Germany. That same year, the Karolis team (named "Flacara"—the flame) won first place in Romania's Women's Gymnastics Championships. That title gave to the Onesti Gymnastic Center the ranking of second-best gymnastic school in Romania, next only to Bucharest's.

THE FOLLOWING YEAR was a "quiet" one for Nadia. In the Friendship Tournament in North Korea, she and her team won the cup after a dramatic competition, despite the fact that Nadia had sprained her ankle during the warm-up and fainted several times from an allergic reaction to the painkiller given her.

She was seen by Americans first in that year when Rodney Hill brought his "Hill's Angels" team to Romania from his Denver School of Gymnastics. The team included his wife, Debbie, an American Olympic champion.

When they visited Onesti, they were greeted by a team of what seemed to them to be little girls. Hill politely suggested that because his wife was, after all, an Olympic champion, perhaps she should not compete—to make the contest more equal. The Romanian coach told him this would not be necessary.

A thirteen-year-old Romanian bested Debbie in three of four events, with Debbie winning only on the balance beam. The Romanian was Nadia Comaneci, who won the all-round competition by five-tenths of a point, with Debbie coming in second. An astonished Rod Hill came to the conclusion, and told everyone on his return to the United States, that Nadia was the greatest gymnast the world had ever seen, or would see, for a long time to come.

For Nadia and her coaches, the "quiet" year was one of her most important as far as training was concerned. The aim of the Karolis in 1974 was not to win more gold medals, but to prepare a solid, modern and spectacular routine for the next major competitive year. It was not good, they decided, for Nadia to chance any risk of failure. Nothing, the Karolis felt, should shake Nadia's trust in herself.

Her gymnastics objective for 1974 was more important than anyone might imagine: she was working toward the Montreal competition! In the modern gymnastics hall of her home town, Nadia prepared new combinations for each piece of apparatus. She put together a new line of executions, she polished her "torrents," her unique style.

The coaching decision was correct. By keeping Nadia in training throughout 1974, they prepared her for astonishing surprises later. Nadia and her coaches discovered new ways to perform on each piece of apparatus, and an endless amount of work was necessary to create and perfect Nadia's routines. The understanding and collaboration between the young champion and her coaches was more than impressive. They knew what they wanted, what they hoped and what they needed to do if their aims were to be achieved. And they succeeded. At the end of the year they demonstrated their burning desire to win on the most incredible day of Nadia's career—her unheralded performance in Paris—when nothing and nobody could stop the girl's talent and her coach's ambition to show their gymnastic fortitude.

On the uneven bars
(*Bob Greene, New York*)

5

Building Toward a Climax

IF 1974 WAS the most important year in Nadia's training, 1975 was surely the most important year with regard to gymnastics victories.

The greatest objective for Nadia was the European Championships that were to take place in Skien, Norway in May. Perhaps it was the early date of that important competition that made the Romanian Gymnastics Federation decide to send Nadia to London in April for the Women Champion's Tournament, rather than have her compete in Romania (on the same date) in Romania's prestigious International Gymnastic Competition.

The leaders of Romanian gymnastics knew how to manage Nadia's program before the European Championships. By competing in London, she would become adjusted to a long air trip, as well as to the feeling of being abroad after the lack of competition in 1974. In fact, London was really a rehearsal for the European Championships at Skien. And she won the "rehearsal" with 37.30 points, as gymnastic specialists the world around labeled her the "wonder child" of gymnastics. Surprisingly, the Soviet Union was not represented in the London tournament by Olga Korbut, Nelli Kim or any famous Russian stars. The U.S.S.R.'s colors were worn by Lyudmila Savina who took second place with 37.10 points. At the tournament, Nadia impressed the jury and audience with her modern style and the precision of her every movement. Meanwhile, Romania's International Competition was won by another Romanian gymnast, Alina Goreac.

ON MAY 3–4, the European Championships took place at Skien, Norway. In Chapter Six we will detail how Nadia took gold medals in the all-round competition; the vaulting, the uneven parallel bars and the balance beam events. Her only "failure" was a silver medal in the floor exercises!

The previous year, with its work, planning and dedication, had been the correct choice for Nadia's life. Having achieved the important victory at Skien, Nadia's next goal was a good performance in Montreal at the pre-Olympic Games. Romania was to be represented by two of Bela Karoli's gymnasts, Nadia and Teodora Ungureanu. It was a major decision for the Romanian Gymnastics Federation to make, and one fraught with psychological danger; for entered in the pre-Olympics were many first-class women gymnasts mentally prepared and physically conditioned for that competition.

If Nadia's place was all but assured, Teodora's place was far from certain. There were many gymnasts with far greater experience than Teodora. But once again, the spirit of the team was very strong. The friendship between Nadia and Teodora, their positive feelings about being together in the same competition, their youth, and their modern "gymnastics line" all contributed to the final decision.

At Montreal, Nadia performed exercises that were newer than those she had used in Skien. That surprised the officials incredibly. Everyone is accustomed to seeing the same routines used for at least one year by each gymnastics luminary. But Nadia was too good to keep the same routines from one competition to the next. She changed a lot of combinations, she put in new executions, she amazed the audience and the specialists time and again—but she couldn't perform at her top level. She had not had enough time to improve everything to the point of perfection, and Nelli Kim won the gold medals for the jumps, floor and beam events. For Nelli it was a kind of small revenge in return for Nadia's triumph in Norway.

Mugging for the camera
(*Bob Greene, New York*)

But Nadia was again the heroine of the pre-Olympic Games, coming in first in the all-round competition and the uneven parallel bars. She won five medals: two golds, two silvers and a bronze. Nelli Kim was the surprise winner at the beam, Teodora was second and Nadia third. The two girls from Romania won a medal on each apparatus, displaying a remarkable level of performance and giving the Russian coaches something to think about for the upcoming Olympics.

Despite her less-than-hoped-for performance in Montreal, Nadia won, for the first time, the title of Romania's "Absolute Woman Gymnast Champion." In that competition she won first place in every event except in the floor exhibition. Nadia's coaches realized that she hadn't reached her zenith and they decided to devote even more time to her training program. For that reason she didn't compete in such competitions as the match between Romania and France, and Romania's International Gymnastics Competition.

Bela Karoli knew exactly where to slow down Nadia's program and how to prevent her from falling into bad habits. Until the end of the year, Nadia worked day after day with no rest except Sundays. Even the Romanian newspapers mentioned that "special attention is being given to training our 'first hope,' Nadia Comaneci."

The Romanian Gymnastic Federation decided that Nadia had done enough for 1975. She had scored victories in everything that could have been won in the world of gymnastics. The Romanians wanted her to be ready the following year to transform a long-held dream into a reality: Olympic gold! And they knew, they were confident that Nadia would take it.

In November the American news agency, U.P.I., accorded her the title of Sportswoman of the Year. She led the world field of women athletes with 263 points. Second place was awarded to Kornelia Ender of East Germany, in swimming, with 259 points. Third place was held by Faina Melnik of the U.S.S.R., in track and field, with 233 points. The "star" of world gymnastics, Lyudmila Turishcheva, placed seventh with 115

Three Romanian smiles as Nadia receives the award for best Romanian sportswoman of 1975 (*Eastfoto*)

points. Neither Nelli Kim nor Olga Korbut ranked in the first ten.

Nadia received the news of the great honor on the day she was celebrating her fourteenth birthday.

THEN THE OLYMPIC YEAR ARRIVED. Nadia's first competition in 1976 was at Bucharest in a match between Great Britain and Romania. She won the competition but she was unable to achieve any "10" scores—her main objective for the year.

Back home, she reviewed all her exercises, working hard to polish each tiny detail of her routines. In February, Nadia and her teammates were on the North American continent competing in Toronto, Tucson, Albuquerque, San Francisco and Denver. The high point of the tour was at Toronto in a match between Romania and Canada. She won the all-round competition with 79.75 points, a record score in the history of women's gymnastics competition. Never before had any woman gymnast scored so many points in an international competition. In her eight events, Nadia was given a 10 six times; once she scored a 9.90 and the other time a 9.85. And the jury for that competition comprised international referees.

After the last competition of the tour, in Denver, the team returned to Romania and Nadia had a chance to rest for four days, during which time she fought off a light flu before flying back to New York City to participate, by invitation, in the first annual American Cup International Gymnastics Competition. She was accompanied by the male gymnast, Dan Grecu, Romania's world champion on the rings. Nadia won the American Cup with a remarkable score—the lowest of her marks was 9.75 for the floor exercise. Her highest score was the now familiar 10, but more of that in a later chapter.

Her next match was between Romania and Italy, and Nadia won the competition with even more points: 79.80.

After the American Cup and a few gymnastic competitions in the United States, Canada and Romania, Nadia took a vacation at a beautiful resort in the Moldavian mountains. Then, on April 23, she started her training again. This time, the training was focused exclusively on routines for the Olympic Games. Bela Karoli altered many aspects of her apparatus routines and changed her floor exercises completely. The floor exercises were also improved for Teodora Ungureanu and the other members of the team. The Romanian coach was making sure, in his training plans, that he would achieve the best form for his students by the second half of July, the period of the Olympic Games.

Before the summer Olympics, Nadia had one major competition—the last "exam" prior to the big trial. In June, Nadia became the Absolute Woman Gymnast Champion of Romania and her fondest dream became a reality for the first time: she scored a 10 for each apparatus in competition. The difficulty of her exercises and the skill and precision of her execution reached the highest levels of her career. Her teammate and friend, Teodora Ungureanu, took second place, having scored a 10 for the balance beam.

A handstand in the split position
(*Bruce Curtis*)

This competition meant much to Bela Karoli and his girls. Nadia Comaneci told Romanian newspapermen: "I worked very hard in recent weeks, pointing to this Master's final because it was to be the competition that would show my best gymnastic form and my possible achievements in the Olympic Games."

Scoring 10s for each apparatus only one month before the Olympic Games gave Nadia (and her coaches) strong reason to believe she would give a good performance at Montreal. They were, of course, seeking at least a gold medal. They could hardly have imagined that, after the first week of the Twenty-First Olympiad, Nadia would be called the "Princess of the Games." But perhaps her coach did.

A youthful star surrounded by even younger autograph-seekers
(*Eastfoto*)

6

The European Championships

BEFORE THE "EUROPEANS" started, Nadia's coaches were able to say with confidence, "We know Nadia's value and we don't doubt the possibility of her winning over both the audience and the specialists."

The audience and specialists, however, were not looking to Nadia, but instead to Lyudmila Turischeva, who they felt would soar to new heights as she had in the World Championships. In spite of major victories, Nadia's name was barely mentioned on the list of favorites at Skien in May of 1975—because the well-known elite of world gymnasts were competing. Surprisingly, Olga Korbut didn't show up; perhaps because of recent injuries, perhaps because she felt it was better to train assiduously for the time being.

In any case, during the warm-up exercises, Nadia's name was on the tongues of audience and referees alike following her spectacular executions. The experts began to realize that Nadia had a good chance of winning at least one gold medal, perhaps more. But the favorite of all was still the good-looking Lyudmila Turishcheva, acknowledged as the best woman gymnast of the hour.

Psychological warfare began between Lyudmila and Nadia, the former clearly realizing Nadia's better form. The Russian's nerves took the strain more poorly than the Romanian's. Lyudmila panicked easily; she was visibly disturbed by Nadia's presence. When the competition began, Lyudmila was more emotional than usual. From the first apparatus event she showed hesitation, even un-

necessary breaks that subtracted vital points from her performance.

By contrast, Nadia started her individual combined exercises with a calm and precision that astonished everyone. Her concentration was perfect, she executed the most complicated movements as if they were minor postures. In the floor exercises, she did her famous two times back somersault with double full twist (720°) as if she were casually performing some ordinary exercise. Her floor exercises were appreciated as the most technical of all and she earned a score of 9.65. From then on, the public was definitely on Nadia's side. Her every appearance was accompanied by gales of applause.

If the floor event was astonishing to the audience, the uneven parallel bars and balance beam brought the crowds to the peak of their enthusiasm. On the bars, Nadia presented two original combinations in a world gymnastics premiere,

Salto Comaneci—dismount from the uneven bars

scoring 9.75 points. On the balance beam, she did her previously unexhibited torrent of acrobatic exercises, again receiving 9.75 points. She also performed a remarkable vault and, after the first day of competition, Nadia held first place with 38.85 points. Second was Nelli Kim with 38.50 points and third, Anelore Zinke of East Germany with 37.95 points. The pre-competition favorite, Lyudmila Turishcheva, ended up in fourth place with 37.90 points.

Nadia and her coach made no comments after the first victory. They were awaiting the second day, which was to be Nadia's greatest real triumph. After she qualified on all four apparatus, she obtained the highest mark of the competition on the uneven parallel bars: 9.90.

For this event Nadia presented a completely new routine from the one she used on the first day. This time she did even better, showing three original combinations that would be named, from then on, "Comaneci's combinations." The audience overwhelmed Nadia with its applause and ovations, and she earned their approbation by scoring two other victories in the horse vault and balance beam events.

Despite her personal and difficult floor exercises, Nadia took second place after Nelli Kim of the Soviet Union. She won four gold medals and one silver. Her teammate, Alina Goreac, took two bronze medals, on the balance beam and horse vault.

Nadia was pleased. Her normally somber face broke into a smile when she took the beautiful trophy of the "Europeans." She was the youngest champion in the eighteen years of the European competition.

Nadia was thirteen and a half when she became an international star. Her popularity circled the globe. The East German newspaper, *Bild,* wrote, "Princess Nadia conquered the world." But the Russian coach, Vladislav Rastorsky, was still skeptical. He told newspapermen: "Until Skien, Comaneci was, for us, an 'enigma.' Now we know her value. It is now our turn to surprise our partners as we were surprised today!"

Was the Russian coach referring to the Olympic Games in Montreal? Was he trying to suggest that somewhere in the Soviet Union there existed a new Russian hope to defeat Nadia? Or had he realized the new gymnastics orientation of Nadia's performance and was he indicating that the whole Russian gymnastics school had to be changed? In any case, analyzing the Romanian's victory, Rastorsky gave the credit to "Nadia's nerves of steel," but he didn't mention one word about the Romanian gymnastic school. Only the correspondent of *Agence France-Press* noted: "The wonder child of the Romanian gymnastics school, Nadia Comaneci, was only one step away from winning five gold medals of the European Championships."

The confrontation at Skien between the two gymnastic schools was not all-out war—the Russian star, Olga Korbut, was missing. Even so, a correspondent for the Reuters news agency wrote:

During a 1976 holiday on the Black Sea coast; training extends even into vacation
(*Eastfoto*)

"In [Nadia's] program there were many elements with so high a level of difficulty that even the Olympic champion Olga Korbut could hardly match it, if she were competing."

The one who cared least about all those matters was Nadia. She made her point very clearly: "I am the European champion because I worked very hard and I have had the best conditions for training myself." And after a few seconds of deep thought she continued, "In the future, I will work with the same seriousness for the Olympic Games in Montreal."

In fact, Nadia said it all!

WHEN NADIA RETURNED HOME, thousands of people were waiting to greet her. The Romanian fans were carrying flags, flowers and posters. One of the posters read: "Bravo Nadia! Go straight ahead!"

In her home town, ready for a good rest, Nadia faced a new problem. In the first few days after the "Europeans," five hundred letters were awaiting replies or at least an autographed photo. Among her fan mail from abroad was a package. An 83-year-old gentleman from England had sent Nadia handkerchiefs, gloves, a scarf . . . and chocolate.

And, of course, reporters from newspapers and TV started to appear among fans from around Nadia's town and other cities.

Nadia answered all her questioners in her very own way:

"What do you think of Nelli Kim?"

"I think she is fine."

"How was it in Norway?"

"Fine."

Her mother was worried about the girl, because Nadia took the price of glory so seriously. Nadia was stopped on the street by admirers at every step and her mother was sure that, had there been a tunnel between her home and her school, Nadia would have used it.

Nadia Comaneci became, in one week, "Nadia," to the world; and, immediately, "Our Nadia," to Romanians.

A new star in the world of gymnastics was rising.

7

The American Cup

THE FIRST ANNUAL American Cup International Gymnastics Competition was scheduled to take place at the new Madison Square Garden, above the busy Pennsylvania Station, on March 27 and 28, 1976. Selected gymnasts from eleven countries were invited to compete for the American Cup. Among the honored guest competitors were Romania's Nadia Comaneci and Dan Grecu.

The printed program made it clear that Nadia was the European title-holder. But the American audiences took a while to determine which of the competitors was the great European champion. In the first place there were a lot of young girl gymnasts, few of whose faces were familiar to the crowds. Secondly, everybody was watching tiny Ilena Davydova of the Soviet Union. Thirdly, and the main reason Nadia seemed invisible, was because the American public was accustomed to the wide, charming smile of Olga Korbut, with her two little braids tied with the large white bows.

Olga had been in the United States a few times, and she had practically conquered the hearts of everyone. Her popularity was beyond belief. Her darling figure was imprinted forever in everyone's mind. The Madison Square Garden crowds were looking for their archetype of a gymnastic star.

It took a while after the warm-up exercises began before thousands of pairs of eyes took notice of the white-clad Romanian with the serious face, who flashed among the other gymnasts from time to time with her amazing movements. She didn't wear her hair in two braids—only a ponytail set-

Cartwheel on the beam
(*Bruce Curtis*)

ting off her bangs. And Nadia's warm-up, as usual, didn't seem spectacular. Most of the time, she conversed with her huge, handsome coach; then she did slow forward bends, hip rotations and some mild stretching exercises.

When a piece of apparatus was free, Nadia went to it, doing some swings or balance exercises. Only a few times did she stun the audience into silence with some unbelievable aerial somersault, or a never-before-seen dismount. When Nadia was doing warm-up routines on an apparatus, she wasn't checking her technique. She was trying out the unfamiliar piece of gymnastic equipment and getting used to the area surrounding the apparatus. She needed some guide marks for her aerial acrobatic torrents, a visual orientation. While the other gymnasts were forcing the apparatus to work, Nadia was flirting with the equipment, asking it to collaborate.

Her white-clad coach followed her performances from a distance. Only in two cases did he come closer to help her; in doing the double back-somersault on the floor, and at the horse vault. A few times when she vaulted over the horse, Nadia didn't land; she remained suspended in mid-air held in Bela's strong arms. It was surprising to see how fearlessly Nadia jumped, even for her first warm-ups, and how well attuned her coach was to preventing her from a mismove. It was surprising, too, the specialists remarked, that of all the gymnasts there, only Nadia knew how to run correctly as she approached the horse.

After each warm-up exercise, the Romanian girl sought out her coach who, most of the time, didn't say a word; he just nodded his head. He too was very serious in his demeanor, almost solemn. No wonder his student rarely smiled. She never sat down, never stopped moving. She continued to do slow stretching exercises. And she didn't seem to pay any attention to the other gymnasts.

NISSEN

Warm-up time was over. Now Nadia offered the American audience the most fascinating and unforgettable performance. They saw the first perfect mark, the first 10 ever scored in gymnastics in the United States. The record-shattering event was the horse vault and Nadia executed a perfect Tsukahara vault. She executed the piked back-somersault as no one in the world could at that time—not even the inventor of that difficult vault, Mitsuo Tsukahara. Ironically, Tsukahara, the great Japanese male gymnast, was also competing at Madison Square Garden in the same meet. He performed his own revolutionary vault and he was scored for the jump with only 9.30 points!

The audience was astounded by Nadia's performance. Her difficult executions, her precision, her talent, all were absolutely out of the ordinary—and beyond the extraordinary. But the American spectators were most impressed by the ease with which she performed her difficult exercises. The same feeling was shared by the referees, officials, coaches and even the other competitors. When Nadia worked at the uneven bars doing her most

brilliant routines, like three free hip-circles to a handstand on the high bar, or her own dismount called "Salto Comaneci," Ann Carr, a top American woman gymnast, called it "madness."

Double back-somersault in the floor exercise

And indeed, "Salto Comaneci" is something special. Nadia swings forward from the high bar, does a half-twist and turns it into a back somersault. After this dismount the American audience rewarded Nadia with a standing ovation. But the Romanian girl didn't react openly to the audience's enthusiasm, and this troubled the spectators. They didn't know how to greet her spectacular performance. She was so serious and she didn't smile. How should they treat her? As a great champion? A wonder child? How to acknowledge a "good job"? Even the judges were troubled; the difference between the Romanian girl and the rest of the gymnasts from the U.S.S.R., Japan, Hungary and Poland was so great that they didn't know to score everybody fairly. The only one who didn't have any problem was Nadia.

She surprised the spectators again with another 10 on the second day of competition. She took the

maximum mark at floor exercises. The event has a little story attached to it. Three times in a row Nadia started her floor exercises and three times she had to stop immediately, because the incorrect music was being played. Three times her coach ran to the music technicians. But the imperturbable Nadia faced the audience with perfect calm, for fully one minute, alone in the center of the Madison Square Garden floor. There was not a sound from the assembled patrons; not a snicker, nor a whisper. The seriousness of the little girl, her somber personality, held the eleven thousand people at respectful attention.

Comedian Flip Wilson, in Romania to film a CBS TV special on Nadia, shows his form
(Bob Greene, New York)

When, finally, her music tape started, Nadia created a sensation throughout the vast auditorium. She opened with her famous double back-somersault. After she completed her floor performance, Nadia was breathing almost normally. But the audience wasn't! A wild cheer of delight accompanied her score of 10 that showed up on the scoreboard. Nadia also won the beam event. In spite of a "low" mark of 9.95, Nadia's performance impressed the audience perhaps the most. They remembered smiling Olga Korbut's beam executions and it seemed to them that nobody would be able to surpass the Russian star. Everybody remembered Olga's arching positions, her back somersaults, her famous split positions and, of course, her infectious smile.

But Nadia did more than that; her aerial cartwheels, her three back-handsprings in a row and her dismount showed a unique, superior way to perform on the beam. And again she was rewarded with a rousing ovation. But there were no fanatic shouts of "Na-dia!" "Na-dia! as Madison Square Garden once echoed with the voices of thousands screaming "Ol-ga!" "Ol-ga!" No one paid Nadia sweet compliments. There was no love affair between the star and the people in the stands. Why? Because Nadia didn't smile at her adulators, didn't flirt with the audience, nor did she remain after each dismount to wave to the cheering fans. When Nadia held the huge American Cup trophy, scores of photographers begged her to smile. And she smiled! Perhaps because she looked at the pho-

tographers' amazed faces. After the competition she was asked many questions by reporters. One of them was whether she was looking forward to the Olympic Games in Montreal. She replied: "I want a gold medal."

Watching the Olympics scoreboard
(*Bruce Curtis*)

"How many?" she was asked. This time she answered, "Five!"

She was also asked what place in the United States she liked the most.

"Disneyland!" she responded in typical fourteen-year-old fashion.

8

Princess of the Games

THE FIRST SPORT on the program at the twenty-first modern edition of the Olympic Games in Montreal was gymnastics. For four days the best women gymnasts in the world performed what might be truly termed a gymnastic marathon in the Montreal Forum. For the first time in Olympic history, the gymnastics competition had to be the most spectacular sport of the Games.

Sixteen-dollar tickets were sold by scalpers outside on St. Catherine Street for $100, even $150. They were the most prized tickets of the Games. All around the world, countless millions of spectators experienced via television the tension of the biggest "fight" in gymnastics history, watched the drama of the most popular women stars of the world in their search for gold and glory—from the beginning to the end. They saw the most brilliant gymnastics competition, one of the most fascinating performances in sports history.

Actually, the interest in the excitement of the gymnastics show at the Forum began four years earlier at the Olympic Games in Munich. It was there that Olga Korbut revolutionized the gymnastics routine when she changed the heretofore "boring" event into a highly spectacular one. Before Munich, gymnastics was never a popular sport. Then the public discovered Olga. Or, better yet, Olga brought to the public's attention the discovery of the new gymnastics.

If the old routines were slow, performed in the main by muscular strength, with endless "unmoving" positions, with almost no perceptible competition except through the jury's measurements, Olga brought to light the spectacular potential of the human body with performances that no imagination had ever before perceived. And Olga led to the discovery that watching gymnastics could be fun, developing in that way the largest claque of fans a star could ever imagine having. She was by far the most fascinating figure of the Munich Games. Yet she was not the best woman gymnast in the world—her teammate Lyudmila Turishcheva was.

For years, the world gymnastic supremacy was owned by one or another of the Russian girls. But in 1975 Lyudmila was beaten by Nadia, then thirteen, in the European championships. Now, at Montreal, these great gymnastics stars were going to compete against each other. Another star performer also had to be counted in: the part-Russian, part-Korean Nelli Kim. She, too, had come to take some gold medals. It was going to be something to be seen, especially after Nadia had so boldly affirmed:

"Olga is just another gymnast for me—nothing else!"

WHEN THE MONTREAL women's gymnastics competition started on July 18 with Compulsory Exercises, Nadia Comaneci scored, on the asymmetrical bars, the first 10 in the history of the Olympic Games, attracting the attention of all the specialists and audience. From then on, she competed in each final of each event. From then on, each time she competed, the TV cameras looked for Olga's and her teammates' reactions, showing the struggle of confrontation between the Romanians and the Russians.

July 19 saw the first real confrontation—but an indirect one. It was the women's team classification gymnastics competition, and it was won by the Russian team with 390.35 points. The Romanian team, the youngest team in the history of the Olympic Games, took second place with 387.15 points.

The Romanians started the competition with the beam event. The second last to compete was Teodora Ungureanu. Her execution was excellent;

A step in the "deep walk," each leg dipping in turn along the side of the beam
(*Joe DiMaggio*)

Another step in the walk . . .
(*Bruce Curtis*)

And another
(*Bruce Curtis*)

she scored a 9.90, and the knowledgeable audience cheered with satisfaction. Nadia was next, star billing, as she performed last for the Romanian team. When she walked up to the beam, a surging murmur was heard throughout the Forum. The crowd sensed something special would be forthcoming from Nadia. And she outdid herself. After her dismount, the scoreboard lit up with a perfect score, the first 10 of the event!

The spectators went wild. They knew there would be a 10, but they hadn't expected it so soon. The Russian gymnasts looked surprised. Olga looked confused. But she cheered up later when Nadia's score in the floor exercises was only 9.85. Her vault was not much better, either. Nadia could be beaten!

But the teams moved on to their next apparatus and Nadia did an amazing routine at the asymmetrical bars, scoring another 10. Now Olga looked even more confused.

The Russians won, but Nadia broke the electronic scoreboards by taking three 10s. No one had ever made a perfect score in the entire history of the Olympic Games. That was why at the next gymnastics event, All-round Competition, eighteen thousand spectators crowded into the hockey palace to see what had never been seen before: a perfect mark, a perfect fight. It was one of the few times the challenge for the title of the best Olympic women gymnasts was not being fought out only between Russians. It was the first time that two gymnastics schools, the Russian and the Romanian, were putting their pride and knowledge on the line; nationalism played a secondary role.

On the first day of competition all eyes were on Olga Korbut and her teammates, greeting their every move. On the second day, everyone in attendance at the Forum was trying to spot the white uniforms of Nadia, Teodora and the other girls of the Romanian team. When the Romanians entered the arena, the rafters rang with the enthusiasm of the welcome.

Everybody, especially those spectators who missed Nadia's first 10s, wanted to see a perfect score again. Everybody wanted to see how the Russian and Romanian girls would react under the strain of competition. But in short order, the all-round event started to be a tug-of-war between two competitors, Olga and Nadia.

Nadia did her vault and the scoreboard showed only 9.85. It was then Olga's turn on the uneven parallel bars and she came through with a big 9.90. The fickle audience returned to their idol and chanted wildly, as in earlier times: "Ol-ga!" "Ol-ga!" She saluted her fans in her charming manner and the crowd went wild. What a recovery for Olga!

Then the drama heightened. Nadia's uneven bars performance and Olga's turn on the beam were scheduled at the same time. But when Nadia started her event, she was the sole performer and her showmanship reached its peak with a most fascinating performance on the asymmetrical bars, as she executed the "world premiere" of three new acrobatic combinations, whirling around the bars, doing perfect handstands on the high bar, finishing with her unique and now-famous "Salto Comaneci."

The crowd was in stunned silence for a few moments after her perfect landing. Then they started to applaud madly. Even Bela Karoli, her usually implacable coach, jumped up in the stands shouting with joy. Another 10 showed on the scoreboard! Bela was quick to sense that her 10 made her a winner. Olga watched Nadia's performance from the other end of the arena, waiting for her turn at the balance beam. She might still win the battle and, for a few seconds, Olga evoked untold emotions from the audience with her amazing body mobility—doing her spectacular curl position, sitting on her chest and bringing her body in a full circle over her head.

Thunderous applause acknowledged her performance and the glory of Munich was again very present in the Forum at Montreal. Many spectators thought Olga would receive a 10, but the scoreboard showed only 9.50. The crowd booed. She sat silently and by herself, her eyes full of tears. She buried her face in her knees. When she finally raised her head, she wiped her face with a towel.

73
73
73

Meanwhile, Olga's coach asked for an explanation from the jury, but the mark was final. Olga had taken too long, exceeding the time limit, and had been penalized 0.25 points.

Olga didn't wait for explanations. She got up and did her vault. Then, not waiting for the end of the competition, she left the Forum floor almost unnoticed by the crowd and headed to the dressing room beneath the stands, wiping her tears. Was it simple coincidence, or the irony of fate that she performed her floor exercise to the tune of "Those Were The Days"?

When Nadia's turn at the balance beam came, the judges awarded her another perfect score! And everyone understood that Olga's dominance had ended!

The 21-year-old charismatic darling took fifth place in the all-round event. She was no longer the star, and she was crying. But Olga's failure didn't mean total Russian defeat. The beautiful nineteen-year-old Nelli Kim performed an excellent vault and took a 10! She also scored a tremendous 9.95 for her floor exercise. Lyudmila Turishcheva scored 9.95 on the horse vault and 9.90 for the floor exercise event, in which she executed a remarkable routine.

But even so, Nadia ran up the highest score: 79.275. She won the gold medal! Her first Olympic gold! Nelli took the silver medal with 78.675, and Lyudmila won the bronze medal with 78.625 points. Much to everyone's surprise, Teodora took fourth place with 78.375—ahead of the impish Olga, winner at Munich four years earlier.

Olympic power and grace at the uneven bars, shown in multiple exposure
(*United Press International*)

ON THE WINNER'S PLATFORM, Nadia received the gold medal in the all-round competition with her accustomed seriousness. But one second later the fourteen-year-old wonderchild thrust up her arms to acknowledge the cheers, shouts and standing ovation—and she smiled at the crowd. She had good reason to smile! Nelli Kim shook Nadia's hand and embraced her before taking her own silver medal. Then, when the great woman gymnast of the world was called for her bronze medal, she walked like a queen, shook Nadia's hand and kissed her before stepping on the platform. Nadia looked very moved at the expressions of such kindness from Lyudmila Turishcheva.

The Romanian anthem crowned the first Romanian gold medal gymnast in the history of the Olympic Games! When the anthem was over, Nadia went to pick up her bag—and her preferred doll. Then she left the arena floor, rushing to meet her coach, who had been sitting in the stands during the competition.

Nelli Kim, Russian silver medalist in the all-round competition, congratulates the winner of the event
(United Press International)

The crowd was leaving too, arguing about the jury's partiality or impartiality, rehashing the performances, commenting on whether Nadia deserved 10s. The Russian coach, Larisa Latynina, was quoted as saying a perfect mark was "unrealistic" because, "Nobody is perfect. Comaneci has her faults too."

But it was too soon to reflect on the competition. Everybody still had fresh memories of Nadia's perfect performances—executions made without hesitation, spectacular flights at the balance beam and the uneven bars. The consensus was that with two 10s or no 10, Nadia deserved the gold medal.

Asked if she had been confident of winning, she answered in her usual forthright manner, "Yes, I was sure." And about Olga's drama? Nadia replied that she didn't feel sorry for her. But Nadia didn't intend to be mean. She knew her own worth, she knew how hard she had worked to be first. She had wanted it so very much. And she won!

The next morning the *Daily News* (New York) filled its first page with a photo of Nadia's aerial somersault, commenting, "Nadia Comaneci flies like an angel during the all-round." The *New York Post* wrote: "Nadia has shown them [jury and crowd] that computers can be wrong and the absolute perfection of a 10 is possible."

From the day Nadia left her home for Montreal, her parents received only one postcard with a view of a church at a nearby community, "Saint Joachim, Pointe Claire." On the other side Nadia

1

wrote, "My dearest Parents: I am in good health. We are living in a big hotel and it is very beautiful here. It is very hot in Montreal. We are working hard and we are all right. You'll see, everything will come up as it should. Kissing you with love, Nadia."

The postcard, which arrived before the competition, didn't say too much, but Nadia's parents knew that she was going to win. Before she left Onesti, her parents were worried about her demeanor: she didn't say a word about the Olympic Games and she seemed more thoughtful than usual, as though unsatisfied with something. After receiving the postcard, Nadia's parents calmed down somewhat. They watched the team competition on TV, and when Nadia took three 10s their belief in her victory was increased. Her father was sure then that Nadia would take a medal in the all-round event. But he was not sure if it would be the gold one. Two nights later, after Nadia's parents saw their daughter's success on TV, the telephone never stopped ringing. And telegrams started to inundate the Comaneci apartment.

People who had never met Nadia's parents called to congratulate them. Notes from officials and private citizens expressed thanks to them for being her parents, for raising such a wonderful child. All Romanians wanted to share in Nadia's parents' happiness. They were recognized on the streets, embraced, and congratulated by total strangers as well as by friends. The next morning, Nadia's father's fellow workers waited for him in front of the plant and sang "Long Life to You" when he arrived, and gave him flowers. Nadia's triumph was everybody's triumph in Romania. The excitement about her gold medal seemed to be the major occupation of every Romanian on those days. But nothing could match the peak of excitement on the morning of July 23 when the finals at the apparatus event were being transmitted on the Romanian TV.

In the Comaneci apartment, the biggest event of everybody's life was about to take place: Nadia's last competition for gold medals. The event was to be seen by satellite transmission at 2 A.M.

Awaiting the post-midnight excitement, Gheorghe Comaneci, Nadia's father, made countless calculations of Nadia's possibilities and predicted that she had less chance of taking a medal in the horse vault. Nadia's mother made an optimistic prediction: she was sure Nadia would take a medal in the balance beam event. She knew from conversations with Nadia that the girl had worked hardest and longest at perfecting the balance beam routine. Adrian, Nadia's ten-year-old brother, declared that he was not going to watch the uneven bars event—he would only listen to the commentary.

Everyone was nervous as the waiting dragged on and on until the 2 A.M. transmission. When the first pictures flashed on the screen from the Forum, Gheorghe Comaneci saw Nadia's figure immediately, and said, "That's my daughter!"

Flying dismount from the asymmetrical bars, ending a perfect 10 performance on the opening day of the Montreal Olympics
(*United Press International*)

The competition started with the horse vault event and Nelli Kim won. Lyudmila Turishcheva took second place. Nadia was fourth. Her mother burst into tears, leaving the room to cry alone. The asymmetrical bars event started, but the TV broadcast switched to swimming events. Nadia's parents, her brother, and all the guests of the family could hardly breathe. It was an effort to calm their nerves. Perspiration poured down their faces. The telephone rang, but nobody heard it. The waiting now was unbearably tense.

All of a sudden, there was an announcement that Nadia had taken first place on the uneven parallel bars. Her mother started again to cry, but this time from joy. Suddenly the TV screen showed Nadia receiving the gold medal. Adrian announced confidently that his sister was a great champion, but she would be even greater because, he assured all, she would win the beam event, too.

The telephone rang and rang, but still nobody heard it. Finally, somebody answered it. Someone from another town wanted to congratulate Nadia's parents. They didn't know who the call was from, but it was somebody very, very happy for Nadia's victory.

Ready to perform, Nadia steps up to the beam (*Joe DiMaggio*)

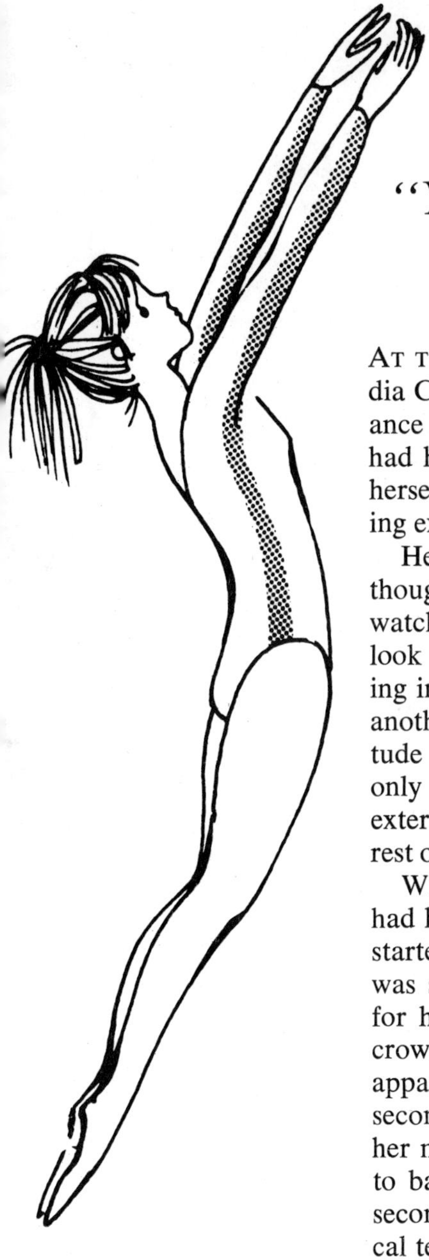

9

"You Deserved a 'Twenty'"

AT THE SAME MOMENT, on the Forum floor, Nadia Comaneci was waiting to perform on the balance beam. Even while waiting to compete, Nadia had her own style. She never sat down, but kept herself busy doing hip rotations and slow stretching exercises, and rubbed rosin into her hands.

Her face showed her serious mien — deep thoughts were going through her mind. She never watched a competitor's executions; seldom did she look up even if a Romanian teammate was working in the arena. Nadia's waiting routine was but another proof that she had the right mental attitude for competition: she seemed to be concerned only about her next performance. There were no external diversions permitted; she turned off the rest of the world.

When she was called upon to perform, she also had her own way of starting her event. She never started until she checked the apparatus, till she was sure of everything being perfectly arranged for her performance, including the noise of the crowd. She always stood stock still in front of the apparatus, looking at it as she reviewed in a few seconds all her upcoming motions, as she felt with her mind and her muscles her effort-to-be, trying to balance it before the action began. Within a second of her first move, all her mental and physical tension vanished. Nadia relaxed totally, ready to accept, welcoming, in fact, the tremendous challenge of winning.

She never started any exercises with apprehension. Now, her name was called, and she stood before a sixteen-foot-long, four-inch-wide wooden

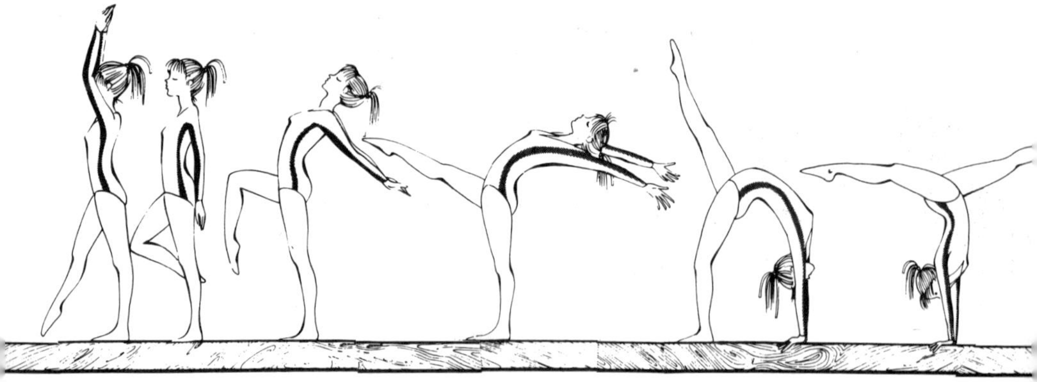

beam. Nadia was ready to start her next performance.

She already had the gold medal for the uneven bars (her favorite apparatus) on which she surprised the judges and the crowd with her unique combinations. But the balance beam was something else. In no other event did Nadia truly show her real potential.

The crowd had seen Olga Korbut doing a back handspring on the high bar, and Teodora Ungureanu almost doing the "Comaneci routine" at the balance beam, but they were about to see the beginning of a new gymnastic era. In no other event is the difference so apparent between the Romanian and Russian schools as it is in the balance beam competition.

Olga's "circus routine" from the Munich competition was once again to impress the jury (and the crowd) in Montreal. She took the silver medal. But Nadia's balance beam performance was completely different from any performance seen before. Nadia barely seemed to touch the beam. Her executions occurred in the air—with perfect landings, without hesitation—an elegant aerial ballet, combining grace with the highest risk of acrobatic

Chain of back-handsprings on the balance beam

torrents. She did presses to a handstand, a one-fourth pirouette and step-down, skips and steps, kicks to a back flip-flop step-out, body waves, down-steps, a pose and an aerial forward, side aerial to a flip-flop step-out, cartwheels to a stand, a back walkover to a handstand in the split position, two flip-flops, a split leap, a round-off, a double-twisting somersault dismount—all as if gravity didn't act on her body.

What she did on that beam, many gymnasts would fear to do on the floor. The rhythm of her elements was extremely rapid, one motion starting another one; but the speed made each execution even more elegant, even more perfect. Her performance on the asymmetrical bars had brought the crowd to express a big "Ooohh!" after the dismount; during the balance beam event, Nadia's aerial flips were permanently accompanied by fierce "Oooohhhs!" As always, Nadia enjoyed competing, expressing the satisfaction of doing such hard work in such an easy manner. Everybody watched Nadia's memorable performance breathlessly. After dismounting, she took one extra step on her landing. That was the only mistake in her entire balance beam routine!

The audience rewarded her with an avalanche of applause; the big ovation almost raised the Forum roof when the electronic scoreboard, under Nadia's number 073, showed that odd "1.00," which in fact, represented the maximum 10 points. It was the seventh 10 scored by Nadia in the Olympic Games.

From his seat in the stands, Bela Karoli lived the most exciting moments of his life. On the winner's platform he twice saw two of his girls take two of the three medals in an event. Teodora Ungureanu finished third in the balance beam event. The silver medal was taken by the 1972 Olympic star, Olga Korbut. Once again, Olga shook Nadia's hand. At the uneven bars Nadia took the gold; Teodora, the silver. Third place went to Marta Egervari of Hungary.

The last event was the floor exercises. Pretty young Nelli Kim took the gold medal. Beautiful, regal Lyudmila Turishcheva took the silver medal. Nadia took the bronze. Her floor performance had been a "special case" for a long time. Sometimes she obtained 10s for her routines, sometimes only a 9.85 or even less. The juries didn't know how to handle Nadia's new style in floor routines. They understood and highly appreciated her personal routines in the other events but, they felt, the floor couldn't be "revolutionized" by Nadia. The demands of a classical routine were still strong and continued to be well rewarded by judges.

Of course, if Nadia had done her double back-somersault, the order of medals might have been different, but she didn't want to risk that much. Her lively floor routine was a theatrical *tour de force,* displaying that new style she had devised—a perfect acrobatic ballet, with surprising stops at which moments she arched one hand gracefully forward and down. Between a chain of flips she danced like no other gymnast had ever done, with genuine emotion and with art.

Maybe itwas necessaryfor Nadia to have smiled more. That might have influenced the judges. Only time will tell if she was misjudged. Nonetheless, she stepped once again—for the final time in the Olympics—to the winners' platform, to be presented with yet another medal. On that single day—July 22, 1976—Nadia scored two 10s, won two gold medals and one bronze. In the single week of Olympic gymnastic competition she won three gold medals, a silver and a bronze, and destroyed the Russian women's gymnastics myth to boot. She didn't succeed in her try to take all the gold medals, but the way she fought for that honor spurred one aficionado to say that "such a fight had not taken place since the Battle of Stalingrad!" Nadia scored seven 10s. Earlier in the competition, a television reporter had asked Nadia how she felt scoring a 10 at Montreal. She answered briefly, "I scored 10s seventeen times before!"

WHEN THE COMPETITION was over, a reporter asked Nadia: "Did you think you could have lost?" She answered, "No! I worked very hard, very seriously; I knew I would win!"

Her coach declared with confidence, "Nadia is the best gymnast in the world."

The Russian women's gymnastic coach, with a touch of scorn in her voice, commented: "If Nadia is really so great, we will see it four years from now in Moscow!"

Awaiting the gold as Teodora Ungureanu, third place winner, applauds her teammate
(Joe DiMaggio)

But Nadia was already a legend at the age of fourteen!

Frank Bare, Executive Director of the United States Gymnastics Federation, commented, "Nadia Comaneci, the youthful Romanian gymnast, has set a new standard of excellence for the sport of gymnastics. She may well have performed so flawlessly in Montreal that the International Gymnastics Federation will have to consider revising its rules for scoring of women's gymnastics. There is no doubt that, based on the rules for judging as they applied at the Olympic Games of 1976, she was indeed worthy of the several perfect scores she received."

The Japanese coach, Yuikio Endo, in tribute to Nadia's performance, stated, "The little Romanian presented her difficult executions so well, with such perfection and artistic feelings, that I understood the big moment of gymnastics had arrived."

And the French coach, Arthur Magakian, said, "For Olga Korbut there existed flashes. For Nadia Comaneci the epitome of expressiveness is there from beginning to end. There are no 'dead' moments in her routine."

Ellen Berger of East Germany, the chief of women's judges, was firmly convinced that Nadia's perfect marks were a realistic verdict. She told the press later, "Nadia's performance was unique and unbeatable."

From the Bulgarian newspaper, *Naroden Sport:* "This delicate, sweet and supple Nadia Comaneci showed us the 'new direction' of Modern Gymnastics. Almost every one of her motions was done as delicately as a jewel. She reached perfection."

The Italian *L'Unita,* noting Nadia's total of 79.275 points out of a possible 80, said, "It is more than a certainty that her score will be a record extremely hard to be surpassed."

The *Times* of London declared that Nadia's name in gymnastics was synonymous with perfection, elegance and masterliness.

The West German reporter from *Die Welt* wrote "Thanks to Nadia Comaneci, the Olympic Games in Montreal widened its dimensions and increased its prestige!"

But the most glowing comments about Nadia's Olympic performance were made, anomalously, by the Soviet magazine *Sovietsky Sport*. Illustrating a report about Olympic gymnastics with Nadia's picture, the journal commented, ". . . Comaneci is, today, indeed the greatest woman gymnast in the world, because she embodied in her program everything modern gymnastics required—complexity, risk, masterly style, emotional élan."

So Nadia became the most popular figure of the Montreal Olympic Games, collecting 10s—and dolls. After the last day of the gymnastics competition she declared, "Today is the happiest day of my life!"

NADIA'S FAME GREW OVERNIGHT, more than anybody could have expected. Nadia's glory in gymnastics was compared with Greta Garbo's in movies. When asked what she thought of her popularity, Nadia answered, with little modesty, "I am a little troubled because of so much attention from all directions, at every step. But I hope that soon people will get used to the fact that an 'absolute' Champion of Europe might win also three gold Olympic medals. . . ."

Asked what impressed her the most at the Montreal Games, Nadia replied, "The soldiers. They were all over the place." And indeed, Nadia was justified in making that statement. The Canadian authorities had remembered the tragic events at the Munich Games and took every precaution to prevent any terrorist attack or incident in Montreal. The biggest concentration of Canadian troops since World War II was brought together to ensure the safety of the competitors.

In spite of all efforts, the Olympic Games in Montreal were marked by political interference. The Canadian government decided not to admit athletes from Formosa unless they were prepared to compete at the Games, not as the Republic of China, but as Taiwan. This conclusion was based on the trade agreements between Canada and the People's Republic of China. Then, less than two days before the opening of the Games, almost two dozen delegations from African countries boycotted New Zealand's presence at Montreal because a New Zealand rugby team (a non-Olympic sport) toured South Africa. Many stars returned to their African homes because of their governments' political decisions.

As in no previous Olympic Games, the 1976 event found itself under greater pressure from nationalistic and political competition than ever. Seeking to win a medal, fencer Boris Onishchenko of the Soviet Union cheated, illegally using an electronic device in his épée to help him score points. Many athletes were accused of taking pills, especially the weightlifters. Others were said to have increased their vitality with transfusions of their own blood. The United States Olympic Committee took a strong stand in deploring political interference in the Olympic Games.

BUT NOTHING COULD cast a dark shadow over the glamor of the Montreal Olympic Games and the Canadian people's efforts in hosting them.

At the opening ceremonies in the gorgeous $650 million stadium, athletes from almost a hundred different countries marched in front of seventy thousand spectators representing more than fifty countries, and saluted Queen Elizabeth of Great Britain, who is also Queen of Canada. For the first time in the history of the Games, the Olympic flame was carried into the stadium by a man *and* a woman, symbolizing all of humankind's achievements. Eighty doves, each symbolizing one year

A press handstand
(Joe DiMaggio)

since the modern Olympic Games started, were released.

From the very first day, memories were being recorded. Who can ever forget the scene at the Montreal Forum when Fujimoto dismounted from the rings: that moment when the Japanese gymnast landed, could anyone have guessed that he had competed with a broken right leg to help his team win a gold medal?

On the same day, Nadia scored three of her 10s, making herself the Queen of the Day. And who will not recall the American men swimmers sweeping up the gold medals, led by 6′6″ John Naber; or the East German women swimmers who gathered in the gold, led by seventeen-year-old Kornelia Ender; or Don Quarrie of Jamaica winning the 100-meter dash, defeating the swift Valery Borzov of the Soviet Union *and* the two American finalists.

For the first time, no American shot putter took a medal.

The United States lost the gold in the men's 400-meter, 200-meter, high jump and pole vault.

The King of the Stadium was still, however, an American athlete—decathlon winner Bruce Jenner, the most handsome all-rounder who decided to end his brilliant sports career to become a movie actor.

Another king, this time of the boxing arena, was Teofilo Stevenson of Cuba, the winner of the heavyweight division at the Munich Olympics, and an absolute winner at Montreal: he finished all his fights before the bell.

The United States boxers amazed the world, with seven of them reaching the semi-finals, a rare performance in Olympic history.

In basketball, Puerto Rico's team lost to the United States team by only one point.

The Soviet women's basketball team won the gold medal—more than likely, because the 7′2″ Yuliana Semyonova intimidated all the other players.

The list of memories of the Montreal Olympics could go on and on, but what happened to Nadia Comaneci after her brilliant Olympic success?

Athlete and coach waiting for the end of warm-up
(*Bruce Curtis*)

THE NEW world gymnastics star didn't wait for the Olympic Games to be over. She was eager to go home because, as she declared many times, she was homesick. The Romanian officials also considered it best for Nadia to leave Montreal, protecting her from the army of reporters. That was a wise decision, because Nadia was tired of being asked the same standard questions over and over. Once she even voiced her annoyance with newsmen: "It is harder for me to answer all those questions than to win a gold medal!" And Nadia needed a vacation after such a gymnastic marathon—she said many times that she wanted to go back to the Black Sea shore for a rest.

Nadia in the Onesti gymnasium
(*Bob Greene, New York*)

On July 27, a Scandinavian Airlines DC-9 landed in Otopeni airport, near Bucharest. Thousands, mostly children Nadia's age, were waiting for "Our Golden Girl," as Romanian newspapers had named her. Almost everybody carried flowers, little flags or huge posters to welcome Nadia and her teammates.

The plane door opened, the stairs were rolled into place, the cheering began; but Nadia didn't appear immediately. A stewardess wanted some pictures taken with Nadia. Finally the Olympic star appeared in the door. The crowd surged toward the plane, breaking through the barriers, everybody trying to give Nadia flowers, or speak with her, or touch her. A singing ovation filled the airport:

"Na-dia, Na-dia Comaneci,
Meritai si nota douazeci!"[1]

[1] ***"Na-dia, Na-dia Comaneci,***
You deserved a twenty!"

Nadia's parents couldn't reach their daughter. After a great deal of effort Nadia was led through the crowd to the airport building. On the way she reached her mother, gave her a big doll and a tender kiss. At every step she signed autographs and answered the reporters' questions.

"Nadia, please tell us what you are thinking this very moment?"

"I am very happy about my gold medals and about this beautiful welcome. I missed my home very much—and now I am hot and I want to drink a lemonade."

"What do you think was the hardest thing in Montreal?"

"Everything was difficult in Montreal, but I worked very hard for my victories and I deserved them. My coaches deserve the same appreciation as I do."

"What do you think was the easiest thing in Montreal?"

"Everything seemed easy for me in Montreal. I knew I would win and I won!"

Nadia's father couldn't take his eyes away from his daughter's medals and he was continually wiping his forehead. The camera shutters and flashbulbs rattled unceasingly, movie cameras buzzed.

"How did you sleep at night before your first gold medal?"

"I slept very well before and after. I think I didn't dream anything."

"Not even about a gold medal?"

"Not even about a gold medal!"

"Were you worried?"

"Maybe I could have been, but I wasn't. I told you that we worked very hard before the Games; our medals are a natural result."

"What will be the first thing you do when you get home?"

"I will take a shower and after that I'll go to bed. I think the trip made me more tired than the gymnastics exercises in Montreal."

"Anything else Nadia?"

"Nothing!"

With five Olympic medals on her chest, Nadia had said everything.

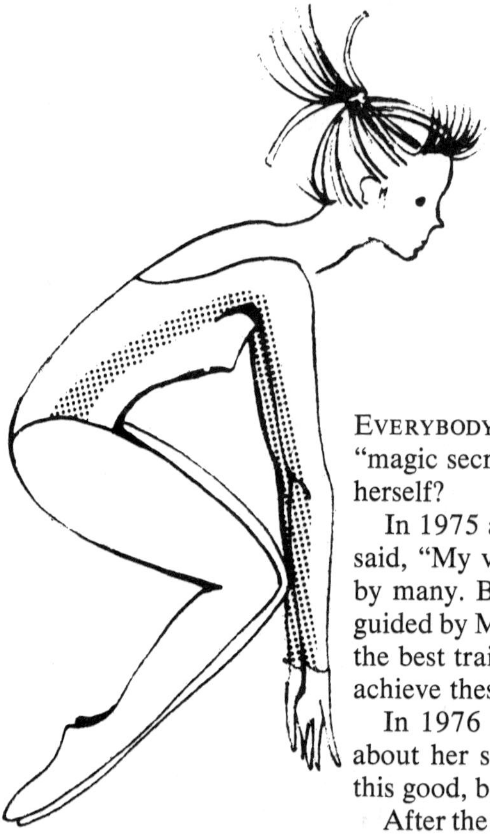

10

Nadia's Secret

EVERYBODY, OF COURSE, wants to know Nadia's "magic secret." Who can tell it better than Nadia herself?

In 1975 after the European championships she said, "My victories may be considered a surprise by many. But from age six I started to practice, guided by Marta and Bela Karoli. I benefited from the best training conditions and I worked hard to achieve these gymnastic peaks."

In 1976 after the American Cup, when asked about her secret, Nadia answered simply, "I am this good, because I work very hard at it!"

After the Olympic Games, in answer to the same question she said: "Of course, at this very moment, I don't think about training, but I am aware, I know very well that after a little time, continuous training, effort and severe work will be awaiting me. Only in this way can I reach the peaks of gymnastic mastery."

The other person who can speak of Nadia's secret is her coach, Bela Karoli. After the Olympics, he said of her victories: "Physically, she has strength, speed and flexibility. Mentally, she has intelligence, phenomenal powers of concentration, and courage." On another occasion Bela said about Nadia's secret: "Her mental attitude is her great plus. She likes to work. She is always the first to warm up. She does everything I tell her."

After seeing Nadia's performances, Frank Bare, the executive director of the United States Gymnastic Federation, stated, "She is capable of doing whatever she sets her mind to do."

Another United States official, Rod Hill, made the clearest statement about Nadia's secret. He said, "She is the epitome of perfection, she has everything going for her—mind, body, discipline, coaches, facilities, flexibility, strength, speed and endurance. What else can you expect but perfection?"

The comments from different gymnastic specialists are endless, but they all express admiration for Nadia's performances. Nadia does not work longer hours than other women gymnasts. She does not expend more energy than any average gymnast but her routines don't come from heaven! In fact, Nadia's training is much simpler than anyone could imagine. That, indeed, could be the "secret."

Seeking to determine what Nadia's true secret is leads to an investigation of her four big qualities: mental, physical, technical and tactical.

MENTALLY, NADIA is the perfect prototype for anybody who needs to have an example set for them. Her gymnastic talent is a happy combination of moral strength, mobility of thought and constructive emotion. Her moral strength includes her seriousness, dedication, tenacity, lack of fear and a tremendous will to win. Indeed, following Nadia's training or the competitions she has been entered in, anyone is impressed by her personality and her serious behavior, which goes deeper than it appears.

By practicing gymnastics from such an early age, she quickly developed a sportsmanlike and personal maturity. Her education was made to serve a precise aim: to be the best woman gymnast in the world. And Nadia *believed,* for such an aim required belief. Due to the great difficulty of practicing gymnastics, her thinking is trigger-quick, very sensorial. For example, the 1/100th of a second needed to accomplish the perfect timing of a grasp, swing or kick, is not a time frame that can be gauged. Many times it cannot even be anticipated. The almost total superiority she holds over other gymnasts is her sixth sense—in Nadia's case, a gymnastics sense, or the "gymnastics instinct." Many times she proved that the instinct existed. If she started a motion and felt it could not be completed right, she would change to another movement, taking advantage of her initial error. She can change a bad body movement into a point-scorer in a fraction of a second. Nadia can improvise anything and no judge can easily guess what her first thought was. That takes perfect concentration and courage and, more than anything else, a lot of self-confidence.

Many experts simply state that Nadia has no emotions. Such a wrong conclusion! She has emotions, but extremely positive ones. Her emotions are not inhibitory, not destructive; they do not cause her to become discouraged. To the contrary, her calm makes Nadia seem to dominate her competitors psychologically—creating a "Comaneci complex." The truth of the matter is that Nadia's warm-up is enough to make any competitor worry.

On the other hand, she doesn't pay any attention to anything happening around her in the gymnastics arena. Nothing can distract her attention from her very own inner thoughts. She knows how to cushion her nerves; she is sure of herself in any situation. Her willpower in competition puzzled the experts. A Bulgarian reporter wrote that at the Olympics it was rather easier to bend a piece of iron than to bend Nadia's will to win. That is not an exaggeration.

Her gymnastic talent is mainly the product of her ability to copy in motion any verbal or pictured suggestion. That, of course, demands a lot of imagination and mental creativity, and perfect motor intelligence in order to control the right muscles. That is Nadia's native gift, but she uses it to its maximum functioning ability. Nadia seems to communicate each 1/1000th of a second with her apparatus. Her physical perceptions coming from her sense of touch as she works on the apparatus are coupled at the same moment with the right responses from her brain, which measures out and supplies the exact amount of strength, speed, etc., to help Nadia act precisely and efficiently. This is the only way her unusual sense of balance and her mathematical precision of execution can be explained. Mimicking so easily and exactly, there is no wonder Nadia can learn an en-

Nadia anticipates her next movement
(*Joe DiMaggio*)

tire routine in forty-five minutes, routines which other women gymnasts need six or more hours to learn. That is the simple explanation of Nadia's remarkable gymnastic progress.

Audiences are always impressed by Nadia's risky performances. But she does not consider them risky. She knows precisely at all times where she is, what she is doing and where she will land. There seems to be a little TV screen in her brain that shows her a fraction of a second in advance what is about to happen. That mental quality is called "power of anticipation."

Nadia has reached perfection because of that anticipatory power, which is based on a sense of orientation and sense of opportunity. Many gymnasts more or less have all these mental qualities. But Nadia's complete advantage is made possible by another mental quality. She can polish an execution or movement in her mind even before working at it. She can sense a mistake before making it and thus can prevent it. Nadia doesn't seem willing to learn a new element the hard way. Moreover, she is not trained just to do *well*—she has been trained to improve a gymnastics routine to perfection.

And we cannot overlook Nadia's important musical sense, her talent to express a tune with joy and artistic feeling. Many a dancer has justifiably commented that Nadia could be a first-class ballerina if she so desired.

Nor can we shortchange her good character. For years she has proved her tremendous dedication and passion to gymnastics and she has been faithful to her commitment. Her coaches developed her in the spirit of the group, treating her with no more nor any less respect that any other gymnast in the class. She learned to respect her teammates equally. During the Olympic competition, the audience was surprised to see Nadia carrying the springboard for Teodora Ungureanu, or adjusting the asymmetrical bars for other teammates.

Between Bela Karoli and his gymnasts there exists a perfect relationship of collaboration and mutual respect. As one wag put it, their relation-

Teodora and Nadia in costume for a dance presentation in Onesti
(*Bob Greene, New York*)

ship is much the same as that between Snow White and the Seven Dwarfs.

Nadia's modesty is a part of her strength of character. Her successes haven't gone to her head, despite the sound of her forthright confidence in herself. That makes her even more brilliant, makes her "secret" even more mysterious.

NADIA SEEMS to have an ideal body for gymnastics: five feet tall and almost 90 pounds. But even at 120 pounds, Nadia would maintain the same gymnastic ability. Her muscles are long and delicate. Nadia looks more like a sprinter or a long-jumper than a gymnast. Indeed, Nadia's physical qualities are superior to those which gymnastic standards used to demand.

Nadia's first physical quality is speed. There has never been a 30-meter dash for Olympic women gymnasts! But she would win such a sprint easily. In the past, classical gymnastic training almost completely neglected the development of speed. That is because gymnastics was concerned primarily with maintaining still poses in difficult positions. Even at Montreal in 1976 the majority of the men and some of the women gymnasts competed in the old manner.

Those who saw Nadia immediately remarked on the unusual speed of her movements, the nimbleness of her highly spectacular routines. Nadia, it seems, was born with speed, and she uses it as the dominant quality of her exercises. Because of her speed, she can do more gymnastic movements than anybody else in a set time frame. Her complicated combinations at the asymmetrical bars, her high and risky vaults, and her double back-somersaults on the floor are the result of her great speed.

Without proper speed she couldn't run as fast or swing as high; therefore, she couldn't "fly" as long or high in the air. She never rushes, but she is the speediest woman gymnast. She is in the air more than anybody else, providing herself with enough time for all her twists and rotations. All those movements underscore her style and make her a winner.

When Nadia competes, she looks much taller than she really is. That is because she has an exceptional amplitude that allows her to fly high, far and gracefully. In film or TV slow motion, one can see that she describes an almost perfect circle in her swings, reaching a maximum radius as she rotates around her point of grip or support. She even surpasses the theoretical line of her body, giving extra stretch from her joints and her points.

Each "fall" on the bar (in the uneven parallel bars event) comes from the maximum height that Nadia can reach with her body, using a perfect extension position in order to increase the amplitude of her movements.

Often when Nadia releases the high bar to fly forward or backward away from it, the audience thinks she has in fact missed the bar. But Nadia didn't miss. Moreover she turned around, flying back and catching the bar on the return—puzzling everybody. That surprising movement is based on a perfect, efficient amplitude. Almost every motion at the balance beam and floor exercises has many momentums when Nadia is in a perfect extension. At the horse vault she uses it as the first aim of her jump. Her perfect amplitude brings grace and elegance to her performance.

Nadia's original style is characterized by her "mid-air flights" and, in fact, she is more often above the apparatus than on it. Exceptional "springability" helps her style. Actually the spring is not only the capacity to jump from the ground as a result of using the feet and legs. In gymnastics, the spring may be effected by any part of the body: wrists, hips and so on. Nadia understands this and utilizes it to maximum efficiency. As she achieves with any other movement, her spring is not an action which starts or finishes by itself. She uses it with design, preparing carefully for every kind of take-off, bringing her body to the best position to favor an ideal take-off. As with all of Nadia's movements, her spring has something a little extra. It is the result of two or more internal "push vectors" which achieve a perfect flight.

A typical example may help explain. The same dismount from the asymmetrical bars at compulsory exercises was executed by dozens of women gymnasts. But only Nadia's dismount was published on the front page of the *New York Times*. That is because no woman gymnast knows how to push with her hips on the lower bar, how to use the best spring. That provides a great plus for her. A ten percent improvement in her spring might add a third of a second of extra flight, which can mean another twist or rotation in the air, thus additional points. Another example: almost all the women gymnasts did aerial somersaults at the balance beam. The then-reigning queen of the gymnasts, Lyudmila Turishcheva, did too. But the difference between Lyudmila and Nadia was patently visible. Lyudmila took off by bending her knees, lowering her body, swinging energetically with her arms, pulling backward with her back and neck, pushing hard on her feet. Nadia did the same execution mainly by using only the spring from her ankles. Her ease of effort was almost discouraging to the rest of the competitors. In the same effortless way she pushed from her wrists at horse vault and floor exercise events. She took off and flew as nobody else.

What really surprises the specialists is that Nadia uses her suppleness so little; much like she avoids using limbering executions. Herein lies her greatest strength, her own point of view in gymnastics: she does not want to use the Russian routine that made Olga Korbut a star at Munich. Nadia does not want to compete on Olga's favorite field. She does not want to be a second Olga.

Nadia does more. She uses her exceptional body suppleness to do her astonishing aerial acrobatic torrents, trying to avoid touching the apparatus except with her palms or feet. In Montreal, Olga Korbut rested her chest on the beam, arching her body backward into a circle, touching her toes to the front of herself. That limber "static motion" was as remarkable in Montreal as it was four years earlier in Munich. Olga amazed the world with her unusual suppleness. But Nadia used even more suppleness in her breathtaking acrobatic flights, displaying a superior way of using the body. The judges were more receptive to Nadia's style than to Olga's, because they recognized that Nadia could have done what the Russian girl did at any time. What was a supreme effort in Olga's limbering exhibition was only a part of Nadia's natural suppleness.

Coordination is a specific gymnastics quality. It is more a quality of nerves than of muscle. A star like Nadia has that quality developed at the highest level throughout her gymnastics schooling. Any comments about Nadia's coordination would be superfluous. Her performances speak for themselves.

Many critics may be tempted to say that Nadia is not strong enough, not as strong as the other woman gymnasts. That is because she does not

display her strength so much during a performance. She does not show that much static exercise in maintaining positions that indicate tremendous muscular effort. Her style almost excludes that kind of exercise, but muscle strength is important to Nadia. She distributes it in a very personal way: when she starts a strenuous movement, she applies her strength quickly at the beginning, and continues her motion with skillful swing, perfect balance and amplitude. At the uneven bars, for example, Nadia does more handstands and grip changes than anybody else; but she does them in such an easy way that she almost appears to be pulled by invisible strings. Knowing how to use her body, she "cheats" the movement, combining her strength with other qualities, achieving better results. After every dismount, her breathing is never hard, nor does she seem to be tired. This is because she does not use her muscle strength for long periods of time; she avoids getting tired quickly. But she uses her additional qualities, es-

Jogging down a street in Onesti
(*Bob Greene, New York*)

pecially the amplitude. It seems as though she is more relaxed than working.

Relaxation is Nadia's most important weapon in competition. It may sound unbelievable, but where other gymnasts grasp the bar or push the hardest on any apparatus, Nadia uses the same momentum for relaxation. She doesn't worry, she doesn't panic, she is not tense about a difficult execution. Her perfect coordination of brain and muscle, of gymnastics instinct and her senses, allow her to use a minimum of effort for a maximum of achievement. She does not miss the smallest opportunity to relax in order to bring about the next step with fresh energy. Her natural relaxation increases the differences between her and other competitors, and helps her to add more new combinations to her gymnastic routines.

Her last physical quality is endurance. Between endurance and relaxation there is a well-known proportional equation: the more time spent in relaxation during work, the greater the endurance. Nadia can practice for hours without need of rest. She can travel all day and night and appear in competition the next morning, fresh-looking as one of her dolls, ready to take first place. Her nature is a perfect harmony of her systems, of metabolism. Few people are born with Nadia's qualities. But she wanted more than that, she wanted to improve. She worked hard and she has improved.

THE INITIAL QUALITY of gymnastics is balance. When Nadia was first seen by Bela Karoli, he immediately saw her unusual sense of balance. And indeed, since then she has amazed the world with that quality which is the result of combining spacial sense, equilibrium, precision and positiveness.

The word "balance" usually leads people to associate with the balance beam, the strongest of Nadia's events. In this event, she has never failed, never even made a wrong step. Her extraordinary execution of the "blind motions" has astonished the sports world. Her three flips in a row displayed more than balance. They showed her power of anticipation in guessing precisely the next spot on which she would land, without seeing it or looking for it. This remarkable sense is the result of her having begun to practice gymnastics at an early age; nothing can be done by other competitors to catch up. Nadia has already handicapped them from the start.

A supersense of spacial orientation seems to be another of Nadia's advantages in her performances. She knows at any moment where she is in the air, how far she is from the apparatus and whether her body is in the correct position. Nadia has never had landing problems or visible flaws in her routines.

Nadia's senses of rhythm and timing are two of her best technical qualities. The execution of a common gymnastics element becomes something special when Nadia is doing it. A simple forward handspring looks like something new, full of spectacular charm and grace. All this because she knows how to wait in the air with calm and natural self-control. Each moment is underscored by perfect body position, superb flight, great dignity. There is no rush, no sign of nervousness or risk-taking—only a magical performance to delight the eye.

Nadia can put together the concept of time, space and movement as no one else. Her excellent rhythm and timing are best seen on the uneven parallel bars, her favorite event. Any swing reaches a maximum elevation when her arms, body and feet are in perfect extension. And her pose is elegant as she goes around the bars, kicking at the last possible moment.

Nadia's handstands are a typical example of her exceptional timing, timing that gives her the best opportunity to perform complicated twists, rotations and flights. In slow motion, one can see she knows exactly when to change body position, how to wait for the best momentum, how to hit the bars at the best time, or to push at the most efficient point of apparatus reaction.

Everything seems effortless when Nadia performs because of her sense of opportunity. On the bars, she reaches a perfect handstand when her

Nadia and Teodora, at ease with the equipment (*Bob Greene, New York*)

swing has no speed left, when it reaches a "dead momentum."

Using the value of the dead momentum is perhaps Nadia's specialty. In any flight or swing she seems to reach both the upper and lower points of dead momentum, making sure she completes her motion thoroughly. Once she reaches the upper one, she stops to check her perfect body position, she even relaxes; in the next momentum she "falls," taking total advantage of free flight as a result of gravitational force. Falling, she prepares her muscles for the next motion by a smooth landing and a short impact on the other bar, going again up into the air for a new reach of dead momentum.

Speaking of gravity, Nadia may be the only gymnast who doesn't fight it, but utilizes it. She knows that putting a brake to the pull of gravity means stopping the landing in a rigid position and failing to reach a lower dead end. Nadia encourages gravity's pull, accelerating her fall in order to use the apparatus and her body like a shock absorber, for a new spring, a new flight. She never puts a hard "break" on the apparatus. Her approach is natural and spectacular. That is why she spends more time in the air than on the apparatus: she acts like a lively ball that bounces higher and higher each time it hits the ground.

Nadia makes the apparatus work for her, not against her. Often during her performances the apparatus seems to move, to go around her rather than she around it. She accomplishes this because she knows how to treat the apparatus well, pushing it firmly but gently, landing elastically, displaying the full beauty of her flight. Even the rigid balance beam seems to help her, as it seems to move under her feet. Nadia knows precisely what each piece of apparatus is capable of offering her, and she never works against the physical possibilities of each. She feels the mechanical forces of it, the elasticity, the right directions to move on it. Nadia and the apparatus are good friends.

All her technical gymnastic qualities are led by her greatest quality: fluency of performance. Many women gymnasts may match individual elements of Nadia's performance, but none can put them together in a routine as she does. The jury of judges in Montreal was most sensitive and appreciative of the difficult parts of her routine, of the risky and unusual flips, but the real reason for awarding her gold medals was her fluency. What she did was so natural and easy-looking, so joyful and charming—her style was unique and superior to any other. The continuity of each of her executions was much like a ballet performance. Each gesture had rhyme and reason; each helped the next; each was a gymnastic recital with a charming, easy manner. There was no worry on her face, no hesitation in her movements, no unjustified stops. It was an acrobatic dance done by the Princess of Gymnastics.

Nadia achieves this form and manner of performance by a simple procedure. She never thinks about the beginning and the end of any motion; instead, she anticipates the next movement, keeping all her personal and gymnastic senses at the alert. In this way she is never surprised by the next step. She feels it before she does it. When she does a torrent of blind back-handsprings, Nadia does not worry about the landing after the first one—she just starts the next back-handspring and continues the chain without breaking a link. Each perfect movement begets the next one, because Nadia does not permit the perfection to be disturbed. She still may make mistakes—but not in her fluency.

NADIA IS the perfect competitor. As in any field, being "the first" is not a one-time thing—it requires re-proof. In sports, especially gymnastics, that proof is difficult to show because being first means not only being the best gymnast; being first also depends on the jury, audience, apparatus, other competitors—and more. Winning first place once might be chance, but winning two times or more requires a level of perfection not easily acquired. Nadia knows how to win and, thus, she knows how to compete.

WHAT ABOUT her coaches' contribution? Before any important competition, Nadia gets special training. Her peak of form must be reached in the week prior to the competition. This precision of objective needs a skillful scientific knowledge of how and at what she should work daily, weekly, monthly—even yearly.

Simultaneous with physical workouts, psychological conditioning also takes place. She is encouraged verbally, to give her self-confidence, to help her trust her coaches, to assure her future success.

Nadia doesn't practice yoga or meditative exercises. In fact, Romanian sports stars do not adhere to any Oriental or occidental practices of this nature. Nadia happens to have a very healthy nature. She has never experienced problems sleeping. She sleeps soundly before any competition. If she worries, she does so in her own style: she will not sit down and she makes sure everything is right before she starts to compete in any event.

The keys to her success are the following maxims:

A watchful moment during work-out
(*Bob Greene, New York*)

- Remember that to train hard is to win easily.
- Don't be concerned about anyone but yourself.
- Be sure about every execution before starting it.
- Show new routines, the more the better.
- Always be ready with a reserve routine.
- Correct a mistake by switching to another movement.
- Do every detail of your performance with expression.
- Treat the risky movements like the regular ones.
- Work fast, but do not rush.
- Create suspense.
- Where others might be afraid, become even bolder.
- Don't show effort, show the beauty of it.
- Put feeling into every perfect biomechanic movement.
- Enjoy your performance and show it.
- Be aware that the audience came to see you, not vice versa.
- Don't copy anybody.
- Someone has to be the best. Why not you?

IN AN EARLIER CHAPTER we mentioned the "Comaneci complex." Nadia's presence in any gymnastics competition sometimes makes the other competitors perform below their best level. A very uneasy feeling passes among other teams when Teodora Ungureanu is scored with 9.90—because everybody knows Nadia is better than Teodora. A psychological defeat, willful or not, takes place. And what is even more discouraging is that Nadia is *always* better than Teodora. Sometimes Nadia doesn't perform her first event well but, where other gymnasts might lose their optimism, Nadia recoups with her highest marks as though nothing happened. Many specialists feel she has no fear. Whether she does or does not is difficult to say, but one can say without fear of contradiction that Nadia is a courageous girl.

Nadia's attitude of reserve is, in fact, her protection against any weakness of emotion. She does not want to get excited about her victories because she is too deeply preoccupied with her gymnastic routines. She is concerned more with work than with victories. Because of her serious attitude and, of course, because of her exceptional successes, an aura of mystery has developed around her. The world seems to feel she has been propelled out of nowhere onto the top rung of the gymnastics ladder as if by a magical force.

Has Nadia Comaneci really come from nowhere?

Nadia Comaneci is a product of the Romanian school of gymnastics.

At the Olympic Games in Melbourne in 1956, the Romanian women's gymnastics team took the bronze medal in team competition. Elena Leustean took the bronze medal at floor exercises and sixth place at jumps and balance beam. At the all-round competition she placed fourth.

In 1960, in the Rome Olympic Games, again the Romanian women gymnasts won the bronze medal in team competition and Sonia Iovan took fifth place in the all-round competition and jumps. She finished in sixth place at the uneven parallel bars and floor exercises.

In the Olympic Games at Tokyo in 1964 and at Munich in 1972, the Romanian women took sixth place in team competitions.

GYMNASTICS IS an important part of the Romanian national sports program. At the National Sports Conference in 1975 the president of the country, Nicolae Ceausescu, said that the sports movements and their people must work to increase the prestige of Romania in international competition, focusing especially on the Montreal Olympic Games.

The Romanian government subsidizes sports heavily. Each town has at least one stadium and an indoor sports hall. Every school and institution bears the inscription in Latin, *Mens sana in corpore sano*—"a sound mind in a sound body"—and the government provides the best facilities for practicing sports for everyone who wants to.

Practicing sports is a lifetime job for most of the athletes and they greatly benefit from the state. Marta and Bela Karoli are among thousands of coaches who constantly search in schools and kindergartens for new talent in all sports events. Early sport specialization by children appears to be the main thrust of sports in Romania.

Romanian sports clubs patronize regular schools, supplying them with sports material and facilities in order to encourage students to attend the clubs' sports activities. From the first grade, physical education is a compulsory subject in all schools—scheduled for at least two hours a week. Many schools have a special physical education program which makes them special schools of sports. The students who excel in sports benefit from the understanding their teachers give them. In North America, a junior basketball star would not be allowed to play with his class team if he was absent from his school too often because of representing his country in his sport; or a star might not be able to compete because he might lose his job. In Romania things are different. At any time of the year a good athlete may leave school or work to go to a training camp or participate in a competition. Sports achievements are rewarded with money and prizes.

Special care is accorded all performers, primarily medical care. Every hospital has a sports clinic; assistance is free. In fact, no one can join a sports club without a medical visa. Medical schools have courses devoted to sports-related medicine and the National Center of Sports Medicine deals mainly with the national and Olympic teams.

Sports events are an important part of daily life in Romania and interest is maintained through newspapers, magazines, radio, TV, meetings, posters, etc. Anyone who wants to practice a sport receives immediate advice and help. As a simple example, in a letters-to-the-editor column of *Sport,* a newspaper, a letter appeared from a group of fourth-grade children from the village of Craciunesti. The youngsters claimed that a girl in their

(*Bob Greene, New York*)

class, Ioana Besliu, was a very talented gymnast. What should we do about her talent?" they asked. The reply was very clear. "You must address your County Sports Committee. She will be helped!"

NADIA COMANECI is now a major star in the gymnastics firmament.

No athlete in the world has her gymnastic experience at the age of fifteen. She represented her country in the International Competition of 1971 when she was only eleven. Her best-known rival, Olga Korbut, competed for the first time on the Russian team in 1969 when she was fifteen!

There is no doubt that Nadia is a new type of woman gymnast. She will change the old conceptions of how a gymnast should look, when one should start practicing, and how one should work. Everything about her is different from the former gymnastic standards for women: her body, her mental attitude about training and competition, and her athletic maturity.

Many women gymnastic stars have seemed to reach a plateau of glory and perfection—Larisa Latynina, Vera Ceaslawska, Olga Korbut and others—each launching a new fashion, a new style in gymnastics. Everyone else has then followed the fashion, dressing and behaving as the current star.

Nadia, however, brought gymnastics to the level of an art. To assist her in her progress, her "team" now comprises two coaches, a choreographer, a physician, an assistant music master and a masseur!

SINCE THE Montreal Olympics, Nadia has been in the forefront of any discussion of international gymnastics competition.

After her Black Sea vacation she again began serious training and, in November, participated in the Balkan championships at Salonika, Greece, where she took the gold all-round medal and four other gold medals, one for each apparatus, scoring a 10 in the horse vault. Later, after an exhibition in Athens, she was presented with a golden commemorative medal.

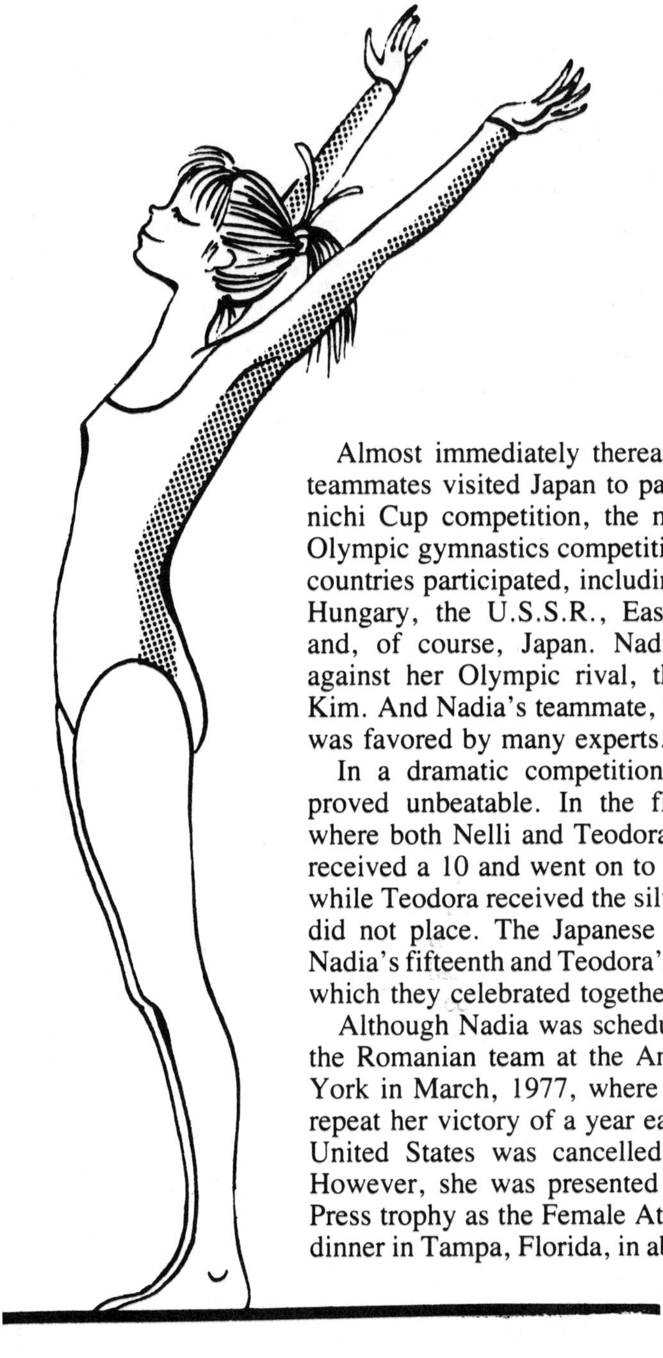

Almost immediately thereafter, Nadia, and her teammates visited Japan to participate in the Chunichi Cup competition, the most important post-Olympic gymnastics competition, at Nagoya. Nine countries participated, including the United States, Hungary, the U.S.S.R., East Germany, Canada and, of course, Japan. Nadia was again pitted against her Olympic rival, the U.S.S.R.'s Nelli Kim. And Nadia's teammate, Teodora Ungureanu, was favored by many experts.

In a dramatic competition, Nadia once again proved unbeatable. In the floor exercise event, where both Nelli and Teodora scored 9.90, Nadia received a 10 and went on to take the gold medal, while Teodora received the silver medal; Nelli Kim did not place. The Japanese visit coincided with Nadia's fifteenth and Teodora's sixteenth birthdays, which they celebrated together in Nagoya.

Although Nadia was scheduled to compete with the Romanian team at the American Cup in New York in March, 1977, where she was expected to repeat her victory of a year earlier, her visit to the United States was cancelled because of illness. However, she was presented with the Associated Press trophy as the Female Athlete of the Year at a dinner in Tampa, Florida, in absentia. She had been a runaway winner in the balloting by a nationwide panel of sportswriters and broadcasters. Soviet gymnast Olga Korbut received this honor in 1972.

Nadia has gained weight and grown taller since the Olympics and this may be creating problems for her. But, in an exhibition in Romania for the benefit of victims of the disastrous earthquake that struck that country on March 4th, she was cheered by a large audience which found her as fit and as spectacular as ever.

What becomes of Nadia in the months and years to come will be demonstrated in competition. Whether she can continue to dominate the sport remains to be seen but, because her ambition is to be a gymnastics coach, she will certainly continue to have an influence for many years to come. There will be new Nadias; her coaches, the Karolis, are training many promising candidates. Every youngster who watches gymnastics wants to be a Nadia, not only Romanian children, but ambitious and talented children from all over the world. And Nadia's words are words they should remember: "I was dreaming with open eyes about a great performance and I have seen that work can transfer the dream into reality."

Nadia's autograph